HEAR US SCREAM

THE VOICES OF HORROR

To request permissions, contact the publisher at contact@hearusscream.com

Paperback: 9780645235500
Ebook: 9780645235517

First paperback edition November 2021.

Edited by Catherine Benstead, S.C. Parris, & Violet Burns
Cover art by Rosie Cass

Published by Hear Us Scream

www.hearusscream.com

CONTENTS

A LETTER FROM THE EDITOR

Dear horror lover,

As I sit here a week out from when this incredible piece of love is due to set off into the hands of those who have supported us so dearly, I am in awe. There is a feeling of love, passion, and empathy that has been washing over me the last few weeks while the editing team and I read through all the essays we have received. There is no feeling like it, it's the feeling of belonging, it's the feeling of being exactly where you are meant to be. That feeling is what these essays represent—they represent all of us.

Horror has given us all a home, it might be a little run down, knife holes in the exit doors, and some blood splattered on the beautiful white tiles in the bathroom; but it is our home. This home houses all of our trauma, our laughter, spirits and friendships. And what a wonderful home it is. Our community is one of the most inviting, supportive, and accepting communities that I have had the honour of being a part of. Without being welcomed in with open arms I would not have had the dream to create something so incredibly special for the community, but especially for our contributors.

Without our incredible contributors exposing their inner-most feelings, their traumatic experiences, and the thoughts that come from the deepest depths of their hearts— this book would not exist. Each and every contributor has poured their soul into their essays to share their incredible love of the horror genre. Not only has this book been created by amazing contributors, but it also would not have made it to the finish line without the support of the editorial team, thank you so much to Violet Burns and S.C. Parris.
Of course the beautiful cover art by Rosie is breathtaking and wonderful!

Never in a million years did I imagine that an idea that I tweeted impulsively into the ether would bring me so much love and joy. I hope that these stories give that to you as the reader.

—Catherine

SQUEEZING MY HAND IN THE DARK: A GIRL GANG I CAN ALWAYS TURN TO

REBECCA MCCALLUM

For much of my life, I have suffered from anxiety, perfectionism, and a crushing feeling of inadequacy. In particular, the theme of loneliness has been a constant—that is not to say that I have been alone (on the contrary, I have always been surrounded by family and friends.)—but I have felt loneliness in all its encompassing and painful darkness at many points and I expect there are many more such moments to come. However, it is through reliving the experiences of women in the genre that I have been able to quieten my mind whilst also fuelling the burning and essential passion that is my ongoing love affair with horror.

From being bullied as a teenager and battling with anxiety as a young woman, to finding how to fit in within the workplace, there has always been a female in horror waiting and willing to squeeze my hand in the dark, acknowledging that I am not going through these life challenges alone. The women I look to within the genre not only offer consolation for the past and ground me in the present, but they fill me with hope for the future. My therapeutic support group might be fictional, but they continually help me to uncover and understand my fears so that no matter how wobbly I might feel, I can find the courage to face each day.

Finding my Inner Power

As a teenager, I was socially awkward, introverted, emotional and over-sensitive. A people-pleaser who sought approval from everyone, when I saw Sissy Spacek in Brian De Palma's *Carrie* (1976) for the first time, a triumphant bang went off inside of me. In *Carrie*, I saw a young woman who endlessly endeavoured to do the right thing and always make the moral choice, credos that I lived my life by each day. However, through watching Carrie's journey I realized that this selflessness in service of others often meant that I sacrificed my wants, needs and desires for fear of upsetting those around me. The perpetual state of terror that pressed on my chest and flicked off a thousand switches of doubt in my brain each time I entered a room or expressed an opinion was both suffocating and exhausting.

When at age fifteen my career advisor asked what my ideal occupation was, my answer was always the same: I wanted to be an author. As cliché as it sounds, books were my friends and a place where I could retreat into alternative realities. Painfully bookish and studious to the point of withdrawal, once I saw Carrie clutching onto her schoolbooks and whiling away her time in the hidden recesses of the library, I immediately knew I was in good company.

Throughout my early teens, I enforced my isolation from others because ultimately, I feared rejection. The loneliness that permeates in *Carrie* felt like an invitation to a group in which I could feel safe and fully belong to. While Carrie is sweet, polite, and smart (qualities that I pressurised myself to fulfil daily through my mercilessly self-critical thinking patterns), she is also drawn to the darker aspects of life through her exploration of telekinesis that is representative of her inner power. Whilst my peers were having a ball hanging out socially after school and during weekends, I took to my room to write essays on Shakespeare's tragedies. This was not homework but work I set myself! The dark nature of the plays presented me with a landscape of emotions, themes, and imagery that I felt intrinsically connected to. From the catalyst of this grew my love and passion for horror, and it was through these associations with the genre that I began to grow too. Just as Carrie finds her power through telekinesis, I too had found my power in horror.

Carrie's closest ally is gym teacher Miss Collins (Betty Buckley), and this relationship felt close to my own experiences as a teenager when I often felt closer and more drawn towards those older than me. Looking at people my own age it was clear to me that I was so far removed from fitting in, so far that no amount of trying would make it so. In her 2019 Netflix documentary *The Call to Courage*, which had a life-affirming impact upon me, researcher and professor Dr. Brene Brown (who specialises in the fields of vulnerability and shame) explained that through her work she had found that 'the opposite of belonging is fitting in' and first and foremost 'we belong to ourselves.' Wise words that decades later I wish I could have bestowed upon my teenage self.

Although Carrie is steeped in loneliness and ultimately has a deeply lamentable ending (a little like the tragedy plays I love so much), there is also a redemptive quality which, on a personal level, makes the film (in parts) a hugely uplifting experience. Carrie may be a target for the popular kids but, unlike me (and many others who have been scarred by bullies), she is able to channel all her feelings of revenge, anger and hurt by harnessing her inner power. I struggle even now to admit this because the cues which push me towards perfectionism and people-pleasing are so strong, but watching Carrie dish out revenge for all she has suffered feels like living the dream, albeit briefly. What I wouldn't give for the chance to stand on a stage in front of my bullies and unleash all hell upon them.

Wobbly and Wounded

Still wobbly and wounded from the bullying, I was also stronger for the experience. After honestly believing at the time that what I had endured would, in one way or another, kill me—I realised that I had made it through, I had survived. The light began to shine and finally, my smile came from a genuine source of inner happiness; I was beginning to find myself. In Sidney Prescott of *Scream* (1996), I found a woman who closely resembled another phase in my teenage years and who I related to due to being a woman older than her years. Importantly, neither her past trauma nor the turmoil she experiences in the film provokes a hysterical reaction from her; in the face of fear, she gets back up again and keeps on living her life. One of the qualities of Sidney's character that resonated deeply with me was her refusal to allow the dark events of her life to define her. Rather than shutting down, a default mode I had retreated into for many years, she gifts herself the time to heal and recognises that part of this is through starting to trust people again. In taking risks, Sidney shows that she is not letting the past hold her back. The bullying I had experienced meant that I felt I needed to hold up a constant shield between myself and the world, but in doing so, I was also missing out on forming friendships, making connections with others, and wrongly gave all the power to the pain of the past. As I made the transition into adulthood I began to sharpen my perspective and (with apprehension and fear) slowly started letting go of defining my self-worth through the opinion of others, something which I am still working on to this day.

11

Women in the Workplace

When I entered the workplace as a young woman, I leaned into the many examples of strong, successful females in horror who took risks and did not allow themselves to be underestimated. The most stand-out example of these is Clarice Starling (Jodie Foster) of *The Silence of the Lambs* (1991). Here was a woman who was not only focused, had found her passion and became the best in her field, but was also vulnerable—in short, she was human. Throughout the film, Clarice is the object of the male gaze, an experience that I feel close to. For over twelve years I was employed as a personal assistant to various Directors and CEOs—with the exception of one, all were male. I lost count of the number of times that I walked into an all-male boardroom to be greeted by a sea of faces not looking me directly in the face but at my chest, legs, and quite frankly, any bit of bare skin on show. To varying degrees, these men deemed it appropriate to touch the skin of my back uninvited, hug me without warning, and on one particularly disturbing occasion fall over my desk in a drunken stupor whilst I was working overtime late on a Friday night.

When asking for a pay raise for my around-the-clock job which one colleague astutely described as "more like care work" than "personal assistant," I was told by a senior representative in Human Resources (who also happened to be a man) that this could not be granted because he deemed the work I was doing to be 'unskilled'. These were some of my formative experiences in the workplace. To this day, I have never recovered from the injustice and sexism that I have watched not only my fellow female colleagues struggling to overcome but that I myself have had to face down on a disappointingly regular basis. It is with all this in mind that I recall Clarice's journey and why I have always had a particular affinity for the moment in *Silence of the Lambs* when she calls out the behaviour of her (male) superior Jack Crawford (Scott Glenn). In typically tactful and yet pointed Clarice-style she does this with politeness and with class; "people look to you to see how to act," she tells Crawford with quiet confidence. Watching Clarice challenge the attitudes and behaviour of those around her filled me with joy and strengthened my own resolve; I wish during my own experiences that I had been able to summon up the courage of Clarice, but I also know that if such incidents were to be repeated in future, I have a new resource in my toolkit.

Alongside Clarice, I came across another incredible woman I could look up to in Ellen Ripley of *Alien* (1979). Playing the role of Ripley, actress Sigourney Weaver described her as "a thinking, moving, deciding creature" (2009, AFI via Alien Press). What Ripley showed me is that being a woman does not mean that you must submit to others and that you can be in charge, in control and be an effective leader. Surrounded by male egos, Ripley is not intimidated by her counterparts and puts the safety of the crew at the heart of all her decision making. Both courageous and vulnerable, I connected with her deeply because I identified with her need for and commitment to survival. As the crew numbers dwindle until finally she is left (not quite!) alone, Ripley remains focused, proves she is highly apt at decision-making and therefore demonstrates that females in the workplace can navigate any problems or challenges they are presented with, even (in Ripley's case) life-threatening Xenomorphs!

When I first settled down in the dark at age fourteen to watch *The Blair Witch Project* (1999), I saw it as nothing more than an effective horror film. However, as the years have passed, I have formed an increasingly strong respect and admiration for the character of Heather (Heather Donahue). Although she may (understandably) be perceived as bossy and overbearing, this is the mode she must adopt as a woman and as a creator to ensure she can be heard. Heather's journey is particularly emotive as she begins with such high ambitions and passion for her project before slowly crumbling, apologising to the group's parents on camera and atoning for her part in the mysterious happenings.

In Heather, I recognised a fierceness, a commitment to her creative project and a drive in making it happen. On the other hand, due to events beyond her control (and as a self-confessed control freak, this was perhaps the scariest component of the film for me), she is also shown in moments of fear and vulnerability. Despite this, she endures some incredibly trying conditions, including hunger and terror while always doing her utmost to remain optimistic and focused. In many of our sessions, my therapist took the care to gently (and repeatedly) remind me that creative people have the greatest imaginations, and the creativity within us can be used as a weapon as well as being our greatest asset. In a constant struggle to keep my anxiety at bay and feed my (ferociously hungry) inner-critic, I plan extensively both mentally and practically for every possible scenario that my head can conjure
up, most of which are extreme and unlikely to ever occur. Through horror, I can play out all these far-fetched ideas, and in Heather, I see someone who faces

life when it throws up unpredictable events that are beyond her control and which no amount of careful planning can prevent. It might have taken me a while to find my coping mechanisms, but now yoga, meditation, and my love of horror—an even balance which I like to think reflects both the calm and more macabre sides of my personality!—are part of a bespoke and essential daily survival kit that I can dip into in moments of crisis. Lost in the woods of Burkittsville, Heather finds her own strategy in viewing the events that unfold through the lens of a camera as opposed to experiencing them as real life, proving that she has the skills of a fighter.

Threatening and Unfamiliar Spaces

More than any other reason, horror pulls me so close because of the theme of loneliness which pervades the films of the genre. Part of a single child household for fifteen years (before my beautiful sister arrived to make our family complete), an outsider at school and in general an introvert who preferred spending time with my thoughts rather than in the real world, it is the portrayal of women taking on trauma, adversity, and threat alone that resonates most deeply and lastingly when I consume horror. The examples of women who have provided me with hope and courage are too large to count and what is more, as I keep broadening my knowledge of horror, the examples continue to grow, urging that frightened little girl within to believe in myself. Whether it's Nancy (Heather Langenkamp) in *A Nightmare on Elm Street* (1984), who draws on her own resources to survive, Laurie (Jamie Lee Curtis) being mercilessly pursued by Michael Myers in *Halloween* (1978) or Jess (Olivia Hussey) waiting alone for a phone call in the sorority house in *Black Christmas* (1974), these films have become a route through which I can channel all my pain and fear whilst simultaneously recognising my self-worth. I may not have endured the ordeals of these characters, but what they are put through serves as a metaphor for the scars and shackles that I carry around with me. Sitting in the dark watching them; I feel wrapped in a cocoon of security, comfort, and empowerment.

The nature of space—both its limits and limitlessness have played a crucial role in aiding me to work through my relentless, stalker-like anxiety. As is true of much of my personal journey with horror, it is through growth, maturity, and reflection that I have been able to unpack my relationship with the genre. My favourite horror film is *The Texas Chain Saw Massacre* (1974); a visual text that deals with notions of being in unfamiliar and threatening spaces. For me, space functions as a metaphor for loneliness and isolation and it is the films that put landscape at their centre which take me to a place of discomfort that feels conversely reassuring.

I consider 2003's *Wolf Creek* to be one of my horror milestones; not least because I still recall literally tasting the terror in the air at the small, poorly attended screening where I first saw it, but foremostly because flashes of the Australian landscape saturated in bright yellow, still creep uninvitingly into my mind years later. In Alexandre Aja's *Haute Tension*, a film that was also released in 2003 and which draws upon my beloved *The Texas Chain Saw Massacre*, the theme of space becomes integral to the experience. As Marie (Cecile de France) travels to the remote sanctuary of the French countryside to study and reset, instead of finding solace, she unleashes a horrifically violent and murderous rampage within herself. Given that loneliness is the scariest thing my mind can conceive of, it is no surprise that it is the films which deal in space that leave me shaking long after the credits roll. Miraculously, they also often manage to find ways of illustrating on screen what I am feeling inside that I cannot verbally articulate.

The Complexity of Motherhood

Now in my mid-thirties, as I look towards the next chapter of my life, I know that there are more women in horror waiting to support me and prove that being older doesn't mean your light becomes dimmer. Horror explores the truth and honesty that comes with being a mother in a way that no other genre can. Furthermore, it does so in addition to eschewing the assumptions around motherhood, providing women with ways in which we can challenge restricting attitudes that have long since expired beyond their sell-by date. I am already able to identify the women who are breaking through such conventions and taboos such as Alice Lowe in *Prevenge* (2017). Through the character of Ruth, Lowe provides a reassurance that when motherhood occurs, it is entirely normal to experience feelings of alienation, a fear that plagues my mind whenever I think of pregnancy.

In *The Babadook* (2014) Jennifer Kent presents a beautifully sad but ultimately healing portrayal of a woman who loses her husband in a car accident. Amelia (Essie Davis) is left a widowed mother to son Daniel (Noah Wiseman) but deep down she wishes her husband had survived in his place. In choosing her husband over her child, the portrayal of Amelia explores a taboo territory that is labelled by many as monstrous and unnatural. As a result of her grief and post-traumatic stress disorder, Amelia experiences a dissociative state and wishes she could return to the identity she occupied before she became a mother. This complexity reflects back to me the dark fears and concerns I have about becoming a mother myself. Within the genre, there are also countless examples of females who serve to illustrate that when women make the choice not to become mothers, this does not mean there are no alternate routes for them to reach their maximum potential and live a fulfilling life. The possibilities that lay ahead for us are boundless and crucially, this does not necessarily include motherhood.

Healing and Believing

Women in horror are given more time, space and in many cases the leading role where other genres do not and this has helped me to uncover parts of myself that I have repressed. In my formative years as a horror fan, the women on screen helped me to find my independence and acknowledge that the most vital and precious resource I have is myself. As I have grown older, the women of horror have continued to guide me towards a refusal to be underestimated and to challenge the assumption that I am not worthy of happiness or success. As I look ahead to potential motherhood and middle-age, I can sit with confidence in the fact that neither of these events means a sacrifice of the core and essence of my authentic self. Whenever I switch off the light, I know there is a hand somewhere in the darkness reaching out to me; I owe so much to my horror girl gang who have helped me to see the blueness in the sky on the darkest days, who have always given me a reason to believe and for bringing a healing power into my life.

LEARNING TO FIGHT LIKE A FINAL GIRL: HOW HORROR INSPIRED ME TO BECOME A WOMAN WITHOUT WOMEN

ZOË ROSE SMITH

Content Warning: suicide

The Strength of Women

They say your early years are the most formative, and that certainly felt true before my teenage years ravaged life as I knew it. There is no denying that I have always been a little kooky and bizarre even as a young child. My parents encouraged this behaviour, as it exhibited my distinct sense of humour and defined personality. According to my dad, in 1996, I spent the year walking backwards. No matter the situation, I was complacent walking backwards amongst the crowds, navigating the world in a completely maniacal sense. But the strange behaviour didn't stop there, as I often wore summer clothes in winter, mathematically divided my food on my plate, and even carried a wooden stake around with me (*Buffy the Vampire Slayer* inspired of course). It's clear to say my parents could tell from a young age that I was self-assured.

My upbringing was fairly unremarkable. There were your typical domestics caused by redundancies, relationship stresses, and financial worries, but these never impacted the way I was brought up—a loving home with loving parents who taught me right from wrong. I spent my first eight years thriving in solitude, with independence and freedom becoming a value that is important to me still. Once my brother was born, I learned to share attention, but it was second nature and needed to be nurtured. This was my first encounter with the ever-changing landscape of growing up.

I always admired my mother when I was young. She reminded me of a living Goddess, one that I felt constantly grateful just to be allowed in her presence. With dark black locks that flowed like treacle, mesmerising green eyes that sparkled in the light and a smile that could eradicate even the most negative feelings, she easily captured the hearts of everyone she met. My mother Emma was fiercely independent and challenging, determined to get what she wanted. My household was considered unconventional, with my mum, the 'breadwinner' and my dad, a stay-at-home carer to my brother. She combined creativity with intelligence, found ways to be strict yet caring, and always felt like the most badass woman that lived in the world. So it wasn't surprising that my grandmother Jessica exhibited similar traits. I came from a lineage of strong-willed yet kind-hearted women.

When it came to my grandmother, you could say I was almost obsessed with the woman; there truly was no one else in the world that I wanted to spend more time with than her. Whenever an opportunity to see her arose, I would beg my parents to drive the four-hour journey so that I could spend my days with her. The memories are fond, and even nearly twenty years later, feel like they happened yesterday. Watching *The Jerry Springer Show,* eating Weetabix in her oversized dressing gown, cuddling up to her on rainy nights when the thunder frightened me. Endless memories that remind me just how much inspiration and admiration I had for the strong and independent woman that I saw.

Angie and Jan were two other strong and influential women who, although they were just family friends, felt like an extension of my blood relatives. They taught me that your power comes from within but harnessing this power can always be executed with gratitude and graciousness. Much like the final girls I would later discover on-screen, they were always there in troubled times: comforting my brother when he needed a friend and becoming motherly figures to me, allowing me to witness their good and bad sides without fear. Through these women, I captured the spirit and ambition of who I wanted to be as a woman—fiercely independent and strong, genuinely kind and caring, with the knowledge of my authentic self.

Death, Decay and Depression

But life doesn't last forever, and from the age of ten years old, I discovered just how devastating loss could be. When I look back on the women, I've lost from my life, my stomach feels empty, steadily filling with a darkness that evokes a sense of drowning. Although there have been films and characters that have represented that, it wasn't until watching Ari Aster's *Midsommar* that my awareness of suffering became more prominent. Even after nearly twenty years since the first loss, my heart still weighs heavy, and my trauma still lingers like an unwanted house guest. After a suicide attempt in 2020, I decided to finally embrace therapy and work through my unresolved past. During these sessions, we worked through the various stages that had played significantly on my mental health, but during each hour there was always one final girl that came to mind, Buffy Summers.

I was first exposed to *Buffy the Vampire Slayer* when I was around eight years old, and watching this badass character really channeled home the traits that were important to me. Two years later my parents broke the news to me that my grandmother had terminal lung cancer. The months were long and painful as I watched the woman who symbolised strength grow weak and frail with every waking day. When they took my grandmother's body from her house, I still remember the zipping of the body bag sounding like a thousand tiny bones being shattered, so loud and piercing yet also sounding like it was muffled underwater. After my grandmother had passed away, my mother became almost an entirely different woman for a long time. She seemed afraid and lost within the world. She had just lost her own final girl, the one who had been her stability and security and taught her strength. I could not bear to imagine her pain, and so I turned to Buffy Summers for courage. In Season 5, Episode 16, Buffy loses her mother to an aneurism. Even though she struggles with coming to terms with this loss, she continues to fight against the oppressive monsters of the world as she continues on her quest to triumph over the darkness in Sunnydale. It was through the strength of Buffy that I discovered my own. I imagined myself as her, supporting my mum with gentle cuddles and reassurance, whilst being brave and fighting the demon that was grief.

Throughout my teenage years, I had my mum, Angie, and Jan, who all influenced me and constantly pushed me to be the best version of myself. I was blossoming into a woman whilst navigating the complicated climate that is adolescence. My tastes were particular, but these three women told me to never be afraid of being confident in my authentic self. Richard Bate Jr.'s *Excision* (2012) demonstrates how liberating being yourself can be. Pauline struggles with her identity at school but begins to realise the power of her true self when she explores her dark sexual fantasies which involve salacious amounts of gore. For a long time, I thought I had to hide my love of horror, especially my indulgence in extremity. Yet Pauline became an example of how pushing past the boundaries of society's constructs can lead to happiness. Whilst my mum, Angie and Jan might not have encouraged bathing in blood, they always supported my need to not fit into a predetermined social construct of how a woman should be.

As a young woman, there is so much pressure to be certain things and do certain things. We're expected to be housewives and mothers, daughters and lovers. We are expected to stay at home with the children, wear pretty dresses, speak eloquently, enjoy rosé and salads, cry at romcoms, the list goes on. But all four important women in my life didn't exhibit those traits—they had careers, they swore, they wore scruffy trousers, they ate steak. They were akin to the final girls I began to see on-screen later in my life once I no longer had their presence in my life. Many years later, once they had all passed away, I watched Adam Wingard's *You're Next* (2018). It was in protagonist Erin (Sharni Vinson) that I found a reminder of the traits that had helped to shape who I was. Without those influential women in my life, I had begun to lose a sense of self. In *You're Next* both the on-screen family and we the audience have preconceived notions of Erin, believing her to be the pretty girl that in any horror situation will succumb to the attacker. But that is far from the truth. Erin is the final girl that no one anticipated, instead brutally slaughtering everyone that dares to try and harm her. This startling yet compelling depiction reminded me of the encouragement given by the deceased women from my life. By seeing Erin use her intelligence to set traps against the attackers and persevere in the face of fear, I remembered that I could be as strong, powerful, and determined as I wanted whilst also wearing that pretty little floral dress.

I was only seventeen years old when my mother was diagnosed with terminal breast cancer. The metaphorical beast had reared its ugly head once more to claim the life of someone special to me. The cancer ravaged her with time, gradually destroying everything that had made my mother the woman she was. There was a sense of relief when she finally passed away. No more suffering, no more pain, and she could finally rest. Depression came creeping slowly and silently, leading to a spiral of self-sabotage and abuse, laced with bouts of destruction, causing chaos and hurt towards myself and those around me. But I found solace in horror films, and comfort in the final girls that taught me to get up and fight grief every single day.

Finding the Final Girl

Coming into womanhood and adulthood after having lost the women I would look to for advice and guidance felt like trying to breathe whilst submerged in a pit of boiling tar. Isolation became a part of my daily ritual. I longed to have an embrace filled with motherly love and to feel seen by someone that could understand my emotions and me. I didn't know where to go to find the comfort I sought, which is when I found the influential women of horror films—providing that female connection I was pining for.

Ellen Ripley from Ridley Scott's 1979 *Alien* became a source of motherly tenderness for me. Without a maternal figure to help me navigate the world, Ellen was an inspiring woman I could look to for behavioural influence. After losing the four women in my life, frightening thoughts of how to be a mother myself have always played heavily on my heart. Who would I ask for parenting advice? Am I woman enough to bring up a daughter? Questions that make me feel helpless and in a state of despair. However, *Alien* taught me that maternal instincts come naturally, and even the most unexpected sources can provide guidance. Even though Ripley was the main source of inspiration, it was through the Xenomorph that my perception of needing women in my life changed. She might be frightening, but her ferocity stems from a natural need to protect her young, something built into her genetics and not taught by humans.

The sense of lost femininity has always been something I have struggled with, and when Angie and Jan passed away in quick succession after my mother's death, that feeling of loss increased. I'll never forget the foreboding sensation that encompassed me in those days—it felt like a fever dream, an out of body experience in which I was merely viewing a tragic tale of melancholy. But the truth was I was living through the loss of important females once more. Those questions on who would shape my feminine side were raised again, which is when I found solace in Julia Ducournau's *Raw* (2016). Whilst it brought on pangs of distress at witnessing the sisterly friendship, the cannibal coming-of-age film reminded me of two things. The first being that influence isn't always needed to be who you truly are, and secondly, that femininity doesn't make you a female. Justine battles against her lust for carnal taste and allows her sister to influence her to embrace it, which helps her discover herself but ends in depressing destruction. But what really resonated with me is how Justine is always true to herself. She is not the portrayal of 'feminine.' She feels uncomfortable in dresses; she gets wasted and acts a mess, and she pees in public. Through Justine, I was reminded that I needed to harness that inner self and could do that just through the power of being me.

It has been a long time since I lost my grandmother, mother, Angie, and Jan. But that does not mean that I do not struggle with my own identity on some days and wish for them to be here to offer a word of advice. Not having influential women in my life is tough, and grief is an emotion that exacerbates that. Yet even after a substantial and life-altering loss, the fight must go on. Anna (Malika Monroe) in Adam Wingard's *The Guest* (2014) never once stops fighting against David, who to me is a representation of grief. Even when her entire family is smitten with the entity, she questions its existence and motive. Anna is similar to Dani (Florence Pugh) in *Midsommar*, constantly curious about her surroundings because battling grief is a fight that makes us hyper-aware and attuned to everything around us. Even after years of losing the women that meant so much to me, that grief still feels like an unwelcome house guest or the grip of a cult. The only way to describe immense loss and grief is like drowning, and waking up every day with your lungs full of water can be exhausting. But Anna and Dani wear their grief on their sleeves and don't allow it to consume them completely—instead, they fight like the final girls they are. That is why even all these years later, I still wake up, put on my mayflower crown and leather boots to keep on fighting.

The Sisterhood of Horror

These on-screen depictions of final girls may have taught me acceptance, compassion, and to fight against the demons, but it is the sisterhood I have found through horror that has been a defining element of my life. Before finding horror I always felt a disconnect with the people around me, and with a lack of female influence, there was always something missing. But through horror, I discovered a sisterhood of women that have been the women that I have needed in my life. Many of them close, some of them further afield, but all of them becoming part of a coven that has provided support, encouragement and connectivity in the times when I needed it the most. They are the inspirations and influences that continue to guide me through discovering my true self and accepting the woman I am. Although my journey into womanhood was devoid of women, for the most, it has been through the horror genre that I have connected with women who often felt the same emotions as myself and allowed me to be open about the person I truly am. This sisterhood of horror has given me back something that I lost when death came ravaging through and eradicating some of the most influential women in my life. My gratitude for the women in the horror community and the ones in films continues to grow and bloom; these are the final girls of horror who have helped inspire me to become the woman I am today, and they are the women I want standing by my side when we fight against any monster that stands looming in our paths.

GOOD SUFFERING

BLAYNE WATERLOO

Content Warning: child abuse, rape, sexual assault

The thing about a lot of horror fans is we've been through some shit. Not that the whole community is some sort of trauma Olympics or anything. But you know when people say, "I don't know how anyone could enjoy watching that?" The "anyone" is us, and for good reason.

Many fans of the genre have experienced such terrifying moments in reality, seeing a werewolf tear someone in half on screen is, quite frankly, cute. Because what's a reanimated corpse out for flesh when you've fought back against an abuser who's terrorized you your whole life? What's a thousand-year-old vampire that can't show its face in daylight when you have had to escape monsters that hide in plain sight? An unkillable, machete-wielding behemoth in a mask really doesn't hold a candle to your body being treated like a public toilet against your will.   A lot of horror fans have trauma they can resolve through the genre, and I'm no exception. There have been instances when our brains couldn't contain the pain we have had to endure, so we've left our bodies completely. Horror waits until the coast is clear, picks you up, cleans you off, and welcomes you to a place where you have not only autonomy, but the notion that nothing you're about to see is real. None of it can hurt you. You've already survived, much like the last person standing on screen. You're a hero just like them, however fictitious, however briefly.

There were so many terrifying events in my childhood that my brain even hid one from my consciousness until I was 29 years old. I knew my step-father was abusive emotionally, mentally, and physically, but I'd suppressed the memory of him being sexually abusive as well. Add this to the shitty cruelties too many people experience— rape, a suicide attempt, a tumultuous journey in the United States behavioral healthcare system, and a partridge in a pear tree— and you've

24

got an exemplary member of the horror community.

I say exemplary because as the horror universe continues to become more gorgeous and inclusive, more studies are revealing that much of its audience is trauma survivors (Brown, 2021). This sounds backwards, because when we think of people with PTSD, we think of either the grizzled war vet or Barbara from *Night of the Living Dead*, a mute, fragile darling who can't take on any more frights. We don't typically associate trauma with the feisty twelve-year-old curled up with a stack of R.L. Stine far past her bedtime.

After I cut my family out of my life and started real, in-depth therapy, I was diagnosed with a Complex Post-Traumatic Stress Disorder. This means that there wasn't just one big, awful moment that changed my brain, but constant, ongoing trauma for years and years, until my brain was reshaped entirely (Gilles, 2018). I never knew where or when the harm was coming from next, and living in that state of fear for so long, a state that I thought was normal, makes it hard to imagine any other way of being.

What's a horror movie compared to never truly feeling safe in your own skin? Horror is where I go naturally. It's like popping my fingers or stretching in the morning. Regardless of clinical theories, however helpful, the horror genre is so much more than a coping mechanism or a security blanket. Horror is me.

What occurs in folks who've endured childhood trauma is called "priming." Priming appears in people with higher levels of cortisol (stress hormone) from a young age. The brain is developing in a continuous state of waiting for the next attack, so its cortisol levels stay high, putting the body on alert at all times (De Bellis, 2014). This is a big way of saying people who grew up scared are anxious as hell and seek out catharsis on their terms. While it seems obvious now how my unconditional love for the genre relates to my abuse, subsequent trauma, and mental illness, at the time I was just a kid who liked to be creeped out. Of course, understanding why we do the things we do is never that simple.

Growing up, my parents enjoyed horror movies, which meant that while we were watching them together, they were in a decent enough mood that my brother and I were safe. No one was getting slammed against walls, slapped, told how stupid they were, or walking on eggshells. Looking back now, it's clear that momentary feeling of safety is in part responsible for the comfort horror brings me now.

It's also evident that I clung to that feeling in situations where I felt vulnerable or responsible for my parents' emotions and reactions. Once in middle school,

I walked through my front door and heard a familiar instrumental number from the living room. In half a second, I recognized it, dropped my backpack, and ran in to find my step-father watching the original Halloween. The room drenched in a rare platinum dash of sunlight and hope. With a grin as wide as my head, I begged him to let me finish the movie before going up to my room for the night. He smiled and agreed. That's a good memory.

I grew up in Mountville, Pa, a small town where the only exciting thing to see before whizzing by on the highway was the seasonal haunted attraction, Field of Screams. Before the new one was built in 2003, the town's elementary school playground was right across the street from the haunt. Sometimes at recess we could see people carrying props—bales of hay and planks of wood for the most part. But one day, closer to when the attraction opened for the season in all its chilly, autumnal glory, I swear I saw one of the employees carrying a fake dead body, followed by a scream track that rang out from one of the buildings, riding a cool gust that promised fun in the near future.

A few years later, when I was in high school, I visited Field of Screams for the first time with a friend. Her dad drove us and was waiting in a nearby parking lot for us to do the hayride and call it a night. But, being teens, it didn't occur to us that the lines would keep us waiting for at least 45 minutes. My friend decided to invite a guy she was talking to and wait for him to show up. I had to be home by 10 PM, but she assured me that wasn't a problem, and her dad would have us back in time.

At 9:45 PM, we were still waiting in a line that felt like a sea of yelling, sweatshirt-wearing jagoffs without a care in the world, and still waiting for my friend's guy to show up. I wasn't allowed out of the house very much, so this was supposed to be a treat for me. I'd idolized this place for years and hyped myself up, and I was stuck in a claustrophobic line with a friend who wanted to hang out with someone else.

I asked her if we could leave and try another weekend, because I had to get home. She said no, that my parents would understand. She didn't know and probably wouldn't have believed me if she did, that this was laughable. The only thing my parents understood was how to antagonize me into obeying them. I called home and tried to explain that we hadn't even gotten halfway through the line, and would it be all right if I stayed long enough to ride the hayride and come right home? No, my parents said. I needed to come home.

My friend didn't want to leave, so I did. I started walking in the dark toward home. I was already late, and I wasn't going to let a bad friend get me in more trouble. The walk couldn't have been more than half an hour, but when I told my parents I was on my way by foot, my step-father picked me up on the side of the road. I was terrified and shaking, my nose numb and running. But I tried, I thought. I tried so hard to do this right. He didn't say a word to me.

When we got home, my mom told me to go to bed, and I nearly collapsed. No outrage. No screaming, or beating or threatening. Their mental, emotional, and physical abuse had taught me that what happened that night was my fault, and I was in for a lashing of some sort. But that's the thing about narcissistic abuse. Sometimes it's not fun if the victim is prepared.

The summer after I graduated high school, I'd "broken up" with a boyfriend my parents had outspokenly disliked for months. It's not always favorable when the person you're trying to control and manipulate is being influenced and gaining self-esteem outside of your relationship. This means that I was still finding ways to talk to him, even though they were monitoring my phone and would not let me leave the house. I spent the three months before college torrenting horror movies in the dark: *Insidious*, *The Exorcist*, *Scream 4*. I lapped them up to ease the constant anxiety and pass the time until I could leave.

A week or two before freshman orientation, my parents figured out that I was still communicating with my boyfriend. They threw my bedroom door open as I sat in bed in the dark, taking my phone and smashing it to the floor. On either side of the bed, they screamed as close to my face as they could. When I told them not to touch me, my step-father strangled me, shaking me by the neck as my mom slapped my head. They left me alone, convulsing with fear, until the next morning when my step-father, a cop, told me to get up and get out of the house. I was not to be there when he got home.

What's a man-eating sea monster when your abusers convinced you you're a whore no one could want?

My boyfriend and his parents immediately agreed to take me in, so I started packing my life up in trash bags and looking for job applications. I didn't know if I could still go to college after my co-signers kicked me out of the house. Just as I was getting ready to leave, my step-father came home much earlier than expected. He came to my room, looked around, and asked if I was actually leaving. He said I should stay. The man who'd just throttled me and unceremoniously disowned me said he didn't mean it, and he wanted me to stay. Of course I did. What would my life be like without his support?

That night, he stood over me as I really did break up with my boyfriend. It wasn't until recently that I reached out to him and thanked him and his parents for a kindness and generosity I hadn't known previously.

When my parents dropped me off at college, they barely spoke to me until they were about to leave, when they told me what a disappointment I was to them. Because who gives a shit about superhuman slashers when you've been hollowed out and left to rot in your own self-hatred?

When a guy took me to see *Jennifer's Body* in theaters on our first date, I was utterly, inconsolably, desperately in love—with the movie. But I'm convinced he wasn't really paying attention to the film's premise, because when we went back to his house afterward, he was horned up on Megan Fox and insisted we have sex. When I said I didn't want to, we struggled on his bed, but he ultimately got his fingers inside me. I left my body. I was Jennifer Check, unhnging her jaw and consuming those who treated her like a piece of meat.

As life continues to take its jabs, **I am Beverly Marsh**, fending off her lecherous dad. **I am Sidney Prescott**, executing her piece-of-shit boyfriend. **I'm Dani**, slowly smiling as she realizes the weight being lifted by the smoke from her betrayers' burning bodies. **I'm Sally**, painted in blood and dirt, laughing maniacally in the back of a pickup truck as my torturer continues swinging his chainsaw into the sunset.

THE (NOT SO) SAFETY GAME OF LIFE

JERRY SAMPSON

Living in Darkness

When I was a kid, I often awoke to my bed shaking. I would lie in the dark and feel the earth as it moved around me, beneath me, on top of me, my blankets still tightly tucked around me from when I first went to sleep, my breath a shallow hiccup as I waited for the shaking to stop. A common image I witnessed in these states was a shadowy figure standing next to my bed. As young as five this would happen, a hulking presence hidden in plain sight, faceless, lurking.

As the episodes continued, I eventually understood what was happening, not an earthquake, or a monster rummaging around under the covers or under the bed, but hypnagogic hallucinations. These sense states occurred as I was going to sleep, and though it often seemed like I'd been asleep for hours, it would be only minutes after I'd shut my eyes before they started.

When I got older, I told my mom about this figure and the coiled snake of terror that wound itself around my belly each time I experienced it. She nodded and said, "the same thing happened every night when I was a kid." My stomach plummeted. The last thing I wanted was for my experience to be reminiscent of her childhood in any way because, as she told me, hers was one of permeating darkness, family secrets, shame, and isolation, and it informed every decision she made and lesson she taught.

I was hyper-aware of the effects those shadowy secrets had on her. And to my mom's credit she did her best to keep me protected from living through the same traumas. But in her attempt to shelter me, she went far in the other direction. After my dad left, when I was around ten years old, my mom's vigilance went into overdrive. Each day after school we began playing the "Safety Games," role playing games in which I'd play myself and she'd play a man, any man, often men I thought I trusted, like my friend's dad or a teacher. She would assume their identity for the duration of the game, and it was up to me to recognize the lecherous or insidious actions they may attempt.

It got to the point where I feared most men, crawling into my shell and not wanting to spend the night at my friend's house or have that one-on-one conversation with my teacher. The fear, one that is ingrained to some degree in most girls due to the basic failings of a society that refuses to hold dangerous men accountable, grew inside of me like a spore in the darkest parts of my imagination. It fed off my stranger danger. This fear sprouted into full maturity as I did, and it forced me to recognize that every new curve invited more and more leers and catcalls. I wouldn't call it a self-fulfilling prophecy; it was simply a fear realized.

Fear was a friend, an abusive one, but one that I could recognize and attach myself to. I didn't have other friends who could understand. But fear understood. Fear told me that my suspicions of that one boy I was afraid to be alone with were justified. Fear told me it would be stupid to walk down that dark alley by myself. And honestly, I don't doubt that fear saved my life at least once. But it didn't stop at real danger; it built everything up to be a threat, so that no matter where I was, I saw darkness. And when one is engulfed in such darkness, it's easy to feel alone, lonely, unable to trust, unwilling to trust.

Horror As a Light

There's a strange, shared delusion about horror in the world of those who hate and judge the horror genre, and I maintain that distrust is the strongest emotion driving the delusion. No matter how many people turn their heads in disgust, it is ultimately the feeling of being unsafe that moves a person to hate horror. Take my mom for example, the same woman who ushered in a young lifetime of fear-based decision making and apprehension, believes horror invites negative energy, that it attracts darkness to you. That's how she truly feels, this woman who created the "Safety Games."

And so, when I first discovered horror, Stephen King's *IT* to be exact, she couldn't understand why I would want to welcome that sort of violence and fear into my life. But I didn't mind that she felt that way. In fact, by the time I discovered myself within the genre, I welcomed the scorn. I didn't have the guts to tell her that I was far more fearful of reality than I could ever be of a book, or that it was her fault I felt so unstimulated by other, less intense works of fiction.

With each new book of evil monsters or wicked killers, the veil of darkness was slowly lifted. I recognized myself in characters for the first time in my young life. I didn't understand how the girls I knew simply existed, moving through the world without anxiety or looking over their shoulders. But in horror, in those books, suddenly I saw characters whose fears were embodied. In *IT*, when Beverly was forced to face Pennywise the Clown and, by proxy, her abusive father, she was able to utilize the power of her fear and overcome her own personal terror.

The characters in the stories didn't always escape the fear alive, but most often they did. There were girls and women who were badgered by the looming shadow of death. They couldn't sleep, perchance to dream, because those dreams could open up their world and swallow it whole. But throughout the scenes branded into my imagination, horror became a mirror that showed me the things I feared and that I could beat them, destroy them, and gain the strength to move forward into that darkness and come out alive on the other side.

If Beverly could do it, I could too.

Horror films came after literature. I was in the eighth grade at a sleepover with a small group of friends. My friend's older sister rented *The Exorcist* and *Scream*, and while *The Exorcist* failed to scare me, even then I was quick to reject the idea of religion-based demonology and possession, *Scream* was another thing entirely. It was late in the night, and the other girls quickly fell asleep during the trailers, but I couldn't, still can't, fall asleep when a movie is playing. So there, in the dark, as the Dimension logo appeared on the screen, and the music kicked in, I faced my first slasher film.

I knew Drew Barrymore, the actress who played Casey Becker; I always thought I looked a little like her. The phone rang. She picked it up and I thought, *why the hell are you talking to this stranger?* It was my first case of, "bitch, hang up the phone
and call the cops!" But soon, my thoughts began to change. My body began to react, and I grew fearful for Drew (Casey really), as the voice on the other end began to reveal his intentions, the very intentions I had always feared. He could see her. He was there, at that house outside of town and away from protection. While my friends slept, I witnessed my greatest fear coming to life on screen. Casey was alone in her house with no one to help her. I remember thinking,

there in the dark, I am alone and there is no one to help me. Casey ran for her life, mere seconds away from the perceived safety of her parents. But despite the proximity to those who could potentially help her, she doesn't escape her fate. The masked (presumed) man chased her until she was close, so close to freedom before plunging the knife into her chest. And the real kicker was the look of recognition as she pulls the mask off the killer. She knew him.

Fuck, I knew it.

I sat there in the dark, in those first fifteen minutes of what would become one of my favorite films (read: not just horror films), my senses on high alert, my ears reaching out beyond my friends' peaceful sleeping breaths for the sound of feet crunching the rocky entryway just outside the house. The film continued and, with my stomach clenched and terror at its peak, I watched as Sydney lived out my greatest fear. But as the fear etched itself into my psyche that night, I had a wonderful realization.

I hadn't actually related to the character of Casey at all. I didn't see myself reflected in the victim, but in Sydney. She had trouble trusting and denied her instincts, making choices that could have killed her, and yet she survived. That night I found my final girl soul sister.

There is no overstating the moment that a young woman finds their mascot in horror. It is powerful. After realizing, much too late in life, that my people, those I connect with the most, are those in the horror community, I discovered an earth-shaking love for my fellow women in horror. Those passionate horror analysts, writers, filmmakers who have all, in one way or another, discovered their own strong selves in the genre.

And while I have since felt an interrelatedness to other "final girls" in horror, from Jennifer Hill (*I Spit on Your Grave*) to Yasmine (*Frontier(s)*), as well as those who don't survive, (Anna in *Martyrs*, Becky in *Henry: Portrait of a Serial Killer*), there is something powerful about that first sense of camaraderie in a fictional character. As scared as I was that night, *Scream* opened up my mind and world to the power of the feminine in horror. It also did this without demonizing sex, which was groundbreaking.

Fear, But Fear Itself
Humans will always be afraid. It's a biological necessity to fear nature and the

elements, but the fear of pain, abandonment, hopelessness, and betrayal feel more recent and attached to a kind of disconnect in society. As we spend more time on our phones and away from interpersonal interactions, it is easier to succumb to the sensation of being alone. And being alone means being vulnerable, as there is no telling what awaits in the wild concrete jungle, ready to pounce and eat us alive. We are driven by fear, controlled by it, yet refuse to allow ourselves to indulge in it. It's almost scarier to acknowledge fear than accept it as an inherent fact of life. It's easier to reject fear with every ounce of strength we have, and as a result we are tired, too tired to ever fight the forces using fear to control us.

I always had an issue with control, or lack thereof, because a past that wasn't my own informed my future. No matter how hard she tried to protect me, my mom infused my childhood with a kind of all-consuming awareness of the potential for victimhood. It wasn't until the discovery of horror that I realized my strength. Others may not understand it, and I used to spend a lot of time defending myself against people whose confusion was expressed in condemnation. And ever more so after I moved into the extreme horror sub-genre.

As always, that which people don't understand becomes a source of extreme scorn. I've been consistently told that I can't be a feminist because I watch rape-revenge films. But there are many faces of feminism, and everyone is entitled to practicing their own forms of self-comfort. The gatekeeping doesn't only apply to men with loud voices on Twitter. It takes the form of those who wish to control what a movement looks and feels like.

I no longer take that type of judgement personally because for me, the discovery of extreme horror escalated the intensity of emotions that I already associated with the genre. Extreme horror pushed me farther than other films in the genre in a way that I understood many others would not accept. I experienced immense catharsis within the genre, and though it was mixed with unease, I was forced far outside of my established comfort zone, requiring me to ruminate on the aspects of extremity that crossed my own boundaries. This discomfort has been important for me on my analytical film journey. The transgressive films of the sub-genre push the limits of cinematic consumption, often placing the viewer in the uncomfortable position of witnessing some of the most brutal and violent traumas that could ever be inflicted on a person. But within many of these subversive acts, there is a strong message about society, inherited trauma, cultural depravity, and human excess.

The films are works of fiction: special effects and diegetic sounds forcing the ear outward, stretching to confirm that those sounds of ripping flesh and vile obscenities couldn't possibly be really happening. Some of the strongest women I know watch horror, and a smaller group join me in my love, or is it just bewildered fascination, for extremity. We are the curious few, exploring a world that, for some reason, has presumably been reserved for men and "perverts."

We all have an inquisitive side; mine simply ponders what the body looks like as it rots from the inside out (*Thanatomorphose*), or what pleasure a woman may attain from eating her own flesh (*In My Skin*), or how it may feel to fall fervently in love with your sibling (*Pola X*). I live for the moment I'm on my tenth watch of *Irreversiblé* and feel the same dread and awe as the first, with the low drone of the 28 HZ background noise stirring the pit in my stomach as I prepare for the heartbreak that coincides with the violence near the end of the film.

While *Promising Young Woman*, where a woman goes on a journey of trying to teach men the errors of their way through peaceful means, appeals to a broad audience, I choose to satisfy my revenge fantasies with *I Spit on Your Grave*, wherein a woman is brutally gang raped then recovers her dignity and rejects victimhood by inflicting gruesome vengeance on her attackers. While mainstream audiences still debate whether *Silence of the Lambs* is actually a horror film, I'll happily watch *Martyrs* for the umpteenth time while questioning the point of life and grappling with my hard earned and much maligned nihilism.

Horror saved me from a life of fear. I no longer avoid looking at shadowy corners, but steel myself to face what may exist there. I've found my true self through horror: my passion, voice, writing, and my strength. And through horror I exist in a place of self-acceptance and joy. At times I feel I've left my mom behind, like I'm in that zombie movie where the hero has to leave the slowest of the pack behind. But the truth is that she wasn't lucky enough to find her way out of the darkness, but I have, and I thrive.

HAUNTING, HAUNTED

VIOLET BURNS

My mother has always haunted porches. She was a smoker who didn't smoke inside. Our porch in North Carolina faced the bus stop, and I've always wondered what lore the local kids wove around her on their way to school. Who was she, the haggard figure with matted hair and yellowed claws, ashing into a Folgers coffee can on the peeling green steps? Why did she look like that? Was she dangerous? Knowing my mother, she probably tried to smile at them. That probably made it worse.

Murmurs and stares trailed my mother as she moved through the world, and I felt each one like a punch. I still wonder if she felt them too, if that's why she learned to hide herself away, surfacing only for gulps of nicotine-stained air. I'd be nothing like her, I vowed as I peeled bits of paint from those steps like a scab. I would never. I would be beautiful. I would be loved. Bus stop kids would never recoil from me in horror. I'd make sure of that.

To call myself sensitive would be the understatement of the century. I didn't know it had a name until recently (Rejection Sensitive Dysphoria, one of the most common and debilitating symptoms of ADHD), but the very *idea* of scrutiny is enough to send me into complete emotional freefall. The imagined possibility of someone else's negative judgment is usually more than I can bear. I've spent most of my life constructing an elaborate veneer, a pretty pink shell to hide in. If I could just be smart enough, kind enough, pretty enough, funny enough—if the shell shone brightly enough, maybe no one would notice the oozing mollusk inside.

Little did I know that ten years later I'd be haunting too, that I'd find freedom in my own monstrosity. I'd find solace in the ugly, oozing, slinking places—the rage. On a whim I auditioned at a local haunted attraction: "scare us," they said, gesturing to a table of props. I don't remember exactly what I did during that audition, but I felt something change inside of me, a cathartic shifting of gears. I felt my worst self, the abject, slithering out of the shiny shell, and suddenly I could breathe, relish the air on my unctuous skin, stretch my horrible antennae. *Look at me, fuckers,* I thought with grim satisfaction, for once happy to be seen. *I'm disgusting. Run away.*

Growing up I hated the stares, but it was hard to blame the gawkers. You don't see women like my mother every day: nearly six feet tall, her pendulous breasts swinging beneath a faded blue kaftan, fetid flip-flops revealing yellow talons, legs carpeted with coarse hairs. Shame burned white hot in the pit of my stomach as she crudely gargled water in booths at restaurants, spitting it with a sickeningly wet cough back into her cup, clutching her hanging left breast.

My apartment in California has a little porch, and my mother haunts that too, exhaling smoke onto pockmarked stucco. She was mostly in bed for the short time she was here, fever dreaming in heavy-duty rubber sheets, leaving gray flecks of dead skin on the headboard like a snake. Her orthopedic shower chair was never used for its intended purpose; she was too stubborn for that. That chair became her smoking chair, and it's lurked in the corner of the porch for years, gathering spiders and bird shit and dust.

Today I tried to throw the chair away, but it was too big to fit into the garbage chute. I dismantled it piece by piece in the reeking hallway: first the perforated plastic seat, then the four steel legs, surprisingly rust-free after years outside. Communal trash chutes are full of gnats, so I tried to keep my mouth closed as I sobbed into the foul aluminum. Piece by piece, I dropped her in, but nothing really happened. Symbolic gestures only work in movies.

My mother is dead now, but I haven't had parents for a long time. In eighth grade, the first stop at the hospital was a little green room with a brown leather couch and too many unopened Kleenex boxes, an anxious social worker hovering near the door. My father had died where he worked, a heart attack while seeing a patient. It wasn't real. My ears stopped working. When they ask if you want to see the body, say no. You can't unsee the waxy yellow thing behind the curtain.

I asked the social worker to take me to the neonatal ward; that seemed like the thing to do, to look at babies. Sad people do that in movies, so I hoped it would work in real life. I felt nothing. I hated the social worker and her pitying glances and her stupid argyle sweater set. I hated the babies, flopping sanctimoniously in tiny pastel hats when the world was on fire.

As I started high school, grief over my father's death took my mother piece by piece, or so I thought. Years passed, and she kept on sinking, a little further every day. What was wrong? This had to be more than depression— dementia? Something was wrong and getting worse. She kept sinking further out of reach. No one listened. My concerns fell on deaf ears, and she kept sinking. Every day there was a little less of her. I didn't understand.

My mother, a former Texas debutante turned hippie earth child in later life, was never one for blending in. When she was still herself, she rocked a bohemian aesthetic, eschewing bras and shaving, her curly silver hair long and wild, a nude, full-figured Gaia pendant around her neck. She had always stood out from the other mothers, whom she snarkily dubbed "the purse people," with their sensible bobs and tailored sweater sets. As a socially awkward child already struggling to fit in, I sometimes resented her fiercely individual approach to personal style. I regret that now. I had no idea what was coming. I wish I had appreciated her when she was still herself.

It's hard to pinpoint when she stopped bathing, but she did— her knees, she said. We had a special bathtub installed, the kind for the elderly with high white walls and an outward-swinging door, easy on the joints. This ergonomic hurdle conquered, my mother still almost never used the tub, her mottled skin beginning to form its distinctive scaly crust. I liked the tub, though; it looked like something out of an old-school asylum. I'd shut the door on myself and sink into the deep, deep well, almost deep enough to swim, and imagine being somewhere else.

The transformation happens slowly as the sun dips behind rows of dusty horse stalls at the fairgrounds. Monsters in various states of undress begin to fill splintery picnic tables in the dirt lot, slamming burgers and chugging off-brand energy drinks. Airbrushed latex looks dreamy in the last blue minutes of twilight. Everything smells like coffee grounds and corn syrup, and I'm waking up.

I hated being home. When I was home, I could be summoned. I dreaded the series of repetitive moans that would call me to her bedside, a dreadful *bahhh, bahh,* bahh with no vibrato: less like a sheep, more like a banshee. This was the signal to scratch her back and rub her neck for however long it took to quiet her. I'd perch on the corner of her musty bed, my eyes on the garish hole in the fitted sheet that never changed, awaiting my orders. As I scratched her back, I'd cringe at the off-white flecks that would gather under my bitten stubs of nails.

As my mother left the house less and less, my world narrowed. I spent most of my time alone, my mother dozing by day in bed, by night in the blue glow of the television. The tri-fold mirror in my room was my near constant companion as I stared, transfixed, dissecting every flaw— my pores, my thighs, the hairs on my arms, my disappointing buds of breasts that didn't match my out-of-control, sprawling hips.

Tonight's cast list is taped to the side of a utilitarian block of a building; I check. Tonight I'm scare acting in Motel Hell, and now it's time for me to change. The cast in all black and non-slip shoes enter the dressing room one by one, and monsters come out. I slip a bloody, tattered Goodwill nightgown over my head, somehow still damp with someone else's sweat from the night before. That's fine.

Before my father died, I largely embraced my status as a consummate weirdo. Fitting in was anathema, basic, selling out. Once he was gone, and with my mother fading, I found myself desperately clawing for a life raft, something that would entice others to stick around. I spent more hours still online, talking to sketchy, much-older people whose intentions now haunt me. The ill-begotten attention filled a void, perhaps several, but it felt better than nothing at all. It's a miracle that I survived my young adulthood, considering the sheer volume of internet strangers' cars I hopped into as a means of escape— anything to get out.

Pennywise's face is half-on, but the nose won't stick. He won't sit still; he's sneaking one last sip of Dew from his Big Gulp before the lips go on. The makeup artist is pissed, but never with me. I always sit still when I'm in the chair. I know how to follow rules, how to please. I close my eyes and let the airbrush paint erase me, soothed by the hiss of the compressor.

But the monster is awake now, and she can breathe— breathe right down your neck.

I'm straddling, crouching over my victim's body, and someone's screaming. Maybe we both are. I strike just to the side of her head over and over until she stops moving. Spine contorted, out of breath, I stagger towards the wagon. They are prey. Snot is oozing from my nose; I'm dripping sweat, but I don't care. This makeup can come off. I'm a fucking monster now.

The theme music fades, and the wagon creeps to the next row, leaving sour wisps of diesel in its wake. We're out of sight now, coughing, and I give my victim a sweaty hand up. We're both buzzing. There's a strange communion in the theater of death.

"Was I too rough? Did I hurt you?" I worry aloud each time.
I wasn't. I didn't. We keep going.

MY BABYSITTER WAS A MONSTER

DULCE MARIA

Childhood can be a strange time for many and for me, the strangeness came in many forms often with outcomes contrasting like laughter and screams. Growing up in a place where beauty drowns out the horrific, this can be expected. Horror impacted me because it came at intervals that highlighted the ties between laughter and screams. Even though at the time I didn't know it, these moments of horrific breakthroughs armed me to survive, and eventually thrive in a place where beauty hides the beast. This wasn't an understanding which came easily to me, of course. I was a young girl subject to the sleepless nights the monsters who visited me from everywhere caused; each one representing a new lesson from which I could learn and continue surviving or be stunned to the point of making myself easy prey for their consumption.

If you were to walk into my office, the signs that say, "good vibes" and "life is beautiful" might generate an eye roll or, perhaps, inspire in you a glimmer of hope. Wherever you find yourself between disbelief and trust, I am confident the last thing you'd think is that a monster sits across from you waiting. See, when people think of monsters, they imagine an obvious difference between themselves and the creature; they might imagine three sets of white eyes, long canines which protrude the mouth, and brute strength necessary to carry bodies to a hidden place. The last image to come to mind is a woman, brown-haired with glasses, that wears hot pink lipstick with a matching blazer. Yet, here I am, and you wouldn't know it from looking at me, but I am a monster. The construct of who I am is perhaps an expected amalgamation of nature and nurture. If we are in some sense or another, where we come from and who we were surrounded by as children, then seeing me as a bright colored abnormality means both nature and nurture have succeeded. In embodying the very forces, I grew up in which were often glittered, tropical, and chaotic, I have managed to gain space on unforeseen grounds with access to a future where more like me will survive and abound.

I was born and raised in South Florida where tv commercials entice outsiders by only showing the beauty of the sunlit beaches, rows of multicolored bridges, high rises, and fun-loving people. The truth though is quite the alternate for many and for me, the reveal started when I was only five years old in the care of my first monster babysitter. I remember how bright the tv was in the dark room. No other lights were on—only the tv. I sat on the floor and to my right sat my human babysitter: a lady whose name and image remain a blurred impression in my memory. She must've been trustworthy otherwise my single full-time working mother wouldn't have left me with her; but the lady, like me, must have been hypnotized by the same image I stared at on the tv.

I sat on the floor, looking up at the tv where a man with a decayed green complexion wearing a red jacket and red pants stared right back at me. The air around him was darkened by fog, and suddenly, he started to…dance. I wanted to turn away but the face looking intently at me, and the bodies which danced in unity, called me to look in confusion through the gaps of my fingers. As "Thriller" played, the lady on the sofa didn't move. She was asleep, perhaps, or maybe she thought it was okay for a five-year-old girl to watch the zombies dance in darkness through her small fingers. I could've made a sound, asked her to turn it off but I was listening to the shuffle of the bones clacking in precision and watching how the young woman on the tv did her best to survive. That night, someone would take care of me and keep me in line, but it wasn't the lady on the sofa; instead, the dancing zombies, now safely back in their tombs and the wolfman who stared back into my eyes, took care of me long before I knew I was one of them too.

I should note how fitting it was to get acquainted with my first monster sitter through music and dancing. After all, I was born in Miami and every night, the city is primed for the possibility of dancing zombies. For me, the music made this earliest memory of a monster one of curiosity instead of fear; I often think this is how I have not only managed to learn from my monstrous caregivers but survived the unforgiving world of glittered horror where humans easily mimic normalcy—and superiority—with false representations that have no mercy for weakhearted curiosity. Thankfully, I learned to continue looking at monsters through the openings of my fingers and in time, I started to understand monsters don't always dance; they can hide their gruesomeness which was an essential lesson for my ability to survive.

Several years after my first viewing of "Thriller", I had another experience that marked my relationship with horror because of how it blurred the lines between real and unreal. I was about 8 years old this time and, to be honest, I shouldn't have crept into the room where the movie played on the tv. However, I thought if I looked through the sides of my hands, the dancing would return but instead, this time, the woman on screen screamed violently as she held onto a gate that sparked with the electricity that moved her body towards death. As I watched this scene from *Pet Semetary 2,* in which the boy watches his mother die while making a movie, my hands didn't protect me. So, I ran away from my secret spot where no one had seen me; I ran to my room, threw myself on the floor against the dresser and cried. I cried until the fear passed wondering why nobody helped the woman as she convulsed in agony; I cried because the loss of my mother started to become a possibility more so than ever before. This time, my reaction most likely resulted from an unconscious knowledge that sometimes the monsters are too busy dancing to get you but other times there is no escape from death. At that age, I knew the images I had seen in pieces weren't real, but I felt the violence of those nerve-shattering seconds in my chest and a hopelessness I couldn't decipher lodged itself into my body where I forgot it stayed with its insidious grip on me. Though time passed, I became hostage to the cries I sometimes heard: terrified, lying in my bed, with eyes open—unable to find the source. I became accustomed to this fright which I couldn't have known was but tough preparation to face what arose next.

Growing up, I lived in apartments, and my friends were often neighbors—girls, dark-haired like me—who, like me, roamed the buildings we lived at unaware of who or what stayed behind some of the closed doors we quietly peeked into. One night, while the grownups gathered and watched another movie, I mistakenly viewed the following: a woman on the tv stands mostly naked next to a statue; chains spit out of the statue and clasp into her skin; she screams, but she doesn't die fast. The woman's skin is gone and what remains is a body of blood, veins and tissue; I cannot look away even as she is eventually destroyed and eaten by the monster in the statue. Suddenly, the moment pauses: Who is screaming? Am I screaming now? No, it's my friend. She's screaming. The lights turn on…the party is over. I believe the woman who died at the gate didn't intend to, but she prepared me for this because I may not have recovered from the terror I took with me that night.

Pins lodged into a white head like clay made mazelike shapes; black-robed attire and a red mouth—hungry for more souls and more flesh. Pinhead from *Hellraiser 3* was the most frightening figure I had seen so far and the one responsible for the destruction of that beautiful woman's body; his hunger was also the one I fixated upon the most and for the longest. Something happened to me that night because I got very sick shortly after and nightmares plagued my sleep. Maybe if I hadn't stared, he would've been forgettable but instead, he stayed with me like a selfish caregiver. I learned a lot during those nights of fear and horror and perhaps, he could've killed me too, but he didn't. Instead, he taught me I could survive frights and that I'd need to if I wanted to live. How did the black-robed killer with a hungry mouth teach me this lesson? By giving my mother and me something to ward off with our own powers. During those nights I laid restlessly and scared, my mother waved an egg across my limbs, over my torso, and above my head because she knew something had caught me; so, she did a limpia con huevo to help me through the frights. I cannot say whether her act was effective or not, but I know eventually Pinhead's image in my mind faded and his grip on me disappeared. El susto was gone. I suppose an evolution of my monster sitters is only expected since as I got older, I grew more accustomed to the division between my reality and the tv screen; but, as any horror fan knows, they can come back again and again, and again.

Whether in your neighborhood or the world, knowing the faces of monstrosity is often the only way to prepare. Perhaps because I was accustomed to the English-speaking monsters of the United States, I was then presented with another figure I had to learn to survive from. She travelled from far to join the list of sitters I had had and came to me through one of the people I love the most. Since this is the nature of these insidious creatures, I now realize how necessary this method was since I may not have met her otherwise. Her image is faceless, with long hair, and she came to me through my older sister who had recently moved to Miami from Peru. The night the monster arrived, my sister had told me her story: María la Marimacha, a young tomboy who wouldn't listen to her mother eventually makes a fatal decision on what should've been a normal errand. Her mother gives her some soles, Peruvian money, to purchase some cow hearts which are typical meats for Peruvian skewers. Instead of making the purchase though, she loses the money in a game with some local neighborhood boys. She panics and decides to go to a local cemetery to take the heart of one of the recently deceased. She takes it home, her mother cooks it, her mother and her sister eat it, but María doesn't. Later that night, María is haunted by a voice that groans, "María La Marimacha, devuélveme mi corazón…"—at this point,

I should add, my sister proceeded to make her voice as deep and drawn out for a full effect of terror—and repeated the phrase a couple of times. María, as far as we know, hears the call and accusation getting closer and closer to her as she shuts her eyes. In the next scene, her mother and sister are screaming at the sight of her body, lifeless with an open chest and a missing heart.

There are several significant details that come from this memory: the story was not played on tv, instead, it was told to me like all ancient stories were once told, and it was told to me because I asked. Even though I thought I would be fine, I was terrified. I wasn't as small anymore, and though my sister was a fun and loving sitter, it wasn't her who stood in the corner of my mind that night repeating the phrase, "María La Marimacha, devuélveme mi corazón...". From her spoken words, my mind created its own images of horror. The girl with long hair and an open chest now asked me for her heart and closing my eyes would not save me—she remained in the room of my mind. I believe this moment has remained with me for so long because it was one of the earliest memories I have of monsters in Spanish. If I had been able to survive the ones who spoke and screamed in English, this discovery meant I also had to fight the Spanish-speaking ones. María's impact not only resulted from her arrival through spoken words but because she was formless, and her physicality depended solely on what was in my mind and in my heart. The screen had power, but this awakening of my sensibilities meant I had to adapt further if I was going to continue to survive. A few words would set off my imagination and create instances that lived in me and were sometimes better than reality and on occasion much worse.

Perhaps it's unsurprising that the next figure I grew up with was one that plagued the dreams of children. The lines blur but this time, I didn't sneak a look. I readily watched how in *Freddy's Dead*, the burned man with a green and red sweater, Freddy Krueger, killed young people one by one. How had I reached the point of confidence that I could not only watch but love the fear which crept into my bones as he tortured a poor young man with a hearing aid and used a gaming console glove to bring real death in life through a game? How had this man with knives on his fingers that had killed little children— amongst other things—arrived on my screen without my hands to protect me? I am sure the new understanding of facing the beast to overcome it came from the others I had known up to that point. Though they were horrific, sometimes they danced, or like Freddy, they joked, and my ability to survive only increased if I managed to look outside and within. Throughout my youth, I stayed with many monsters, and I didn't know why. As I grew older, curiosity compelled me to seek them out, and confidence that I could face the figure I had sought started to intermingle with my questions. Although I would not advise anyone to leave their children with monsters, it worked for me because I soon learned, I was one as well.

A little older, I was now different than the five-year-old who peeked at the dancing zombies; I started to seek and want the same power the monsters had. I had learned a lot from their presence, and I wanted to know more; eventually, I came to the next phase of my education. When I asked my sister for a scary story or sought Freddy, I was no longer a passive element in this relationship I had with horror. So, when I heard there was a movie about witches who had powers to change their lives, I knew I had to see these monstrous beings. Imagine being eleven years old, perhaps almost twelve, wanting to learn how four teenage girls grew into their power so well they got what they wanted: love, beauty, fortune, family. The first time I watched *The Craft*, I had expected witches to creep onto my screen in lizard green skin with claws sharp and long enough to eat up all the plump children. Instead, they were four beautiful girls, each different, with a different set of problems, and powers they were growing more confident to use. What I learned from these four witches—Bonnie, Nancy, Rochelle, and Sarah —was that I too could cause eyes to close in fear. While I had been incapable when I was small to fend for myself against the terrors, I now moved from fear to love and admiration for the monsters on my screen. At the young age of twelve, I finally learned that I too am a monster—that I too am a weirdo.

Curiosity is unforgiving. At times, curiosity can bring many rewards while others, you may not be able to handle what you sought out. I am fortunate to say that these moments of curiosity made me more capable at handling the unexpected. Monsters are, after all, the unexpected, the unknown, and that is their power. If I hadn't grown up with my monster sitters, I couldn't have handled the shocks that often came my way. What I learned from seeing Pinhead or Freddy, and the others is that eventually, their strengths can be taken away. The dancing zombies eventually return to their tombs, and Pinhead is called back to the box. Freddy eventually disappears when Nancy faces him, and the ruthless witches lose their powers too. Power is not often given, but it can be taken, and this is what I did. I took the lessons from my monster sitters and became the unexpected because growing up, I could have become what others meant for me to become—prey. Instead, I used what I learned from my monster sitters to survive, but unlike them, I continue to thrive. Still, without them, I may not have realized that I too have power and, like a vampire, can choose who I decide to share it with.

Twenty-five years have passed since I turned to rather than away from the figures of fear. Perhaps, during those last ones, I was not only more confident because I was older but less afraid of the glittering terrors of the palm-treed city. After everything, the images which remain are joined by feelings of darkness and hilarity that only horror can produce. By embracing the blur of what has terrified and compelled me, I learned to hold onto and face the monster. Little by little though, as their power faded, mine grew and now I am the one others should worry about. The clarity in learning that I too could captivate and push to action and empowerment has not escaped me. As I continue drawing on the tactics of survival, horror stories on-screen or in words have shown me, I work to show these empowering steps to others. Although they may not immediately know the fear or worry they carry is surmountable, I pique their curiosity. Like the monsters who sometimes dance or crawl into our vision, that moment may be scary. However, facing monsters can reward with such understanding of the self that the only natural way forward is through a self-embrace that feeds your belly and nourishes your soul.

AT HOME WITH MONSTERS

GENA RADCLIFFE

Whenever I used to be asked what the first movie I remember seeing in a theater was, I lied and said it was Star Wars. I have no idea if I saw it in a theater. I feel like I did. It's certainly plausible. But feeling isn't the same thing as remembering.

It was actually *Halloween*. I was six.

In addition to being rather young when I was born, my parents neither particularly wanted children, nor knew what to do with them. At a minimum, they didn't think anything needed to change about their lives. This was in keeping with a thankfully brief period during the 70s when hippie Boomer parents decided that the best way to raise a child was to treat them like a miniature adult (because it taught resilience and self-reliance, or something). There was no need for my father to stop selling weed out of our apartment, or for my mother to share intimate details of their relationship in my presence. They didn't feel it was necessary to leave me at home when they went out to the movies, even though my grandparents offered to babysit. I'm sure I saw a lot of movies I had no business seeing. *Halloween* just happens to be the first one I remember.

I don't remember being scared by it, although I must have been because I find it scary now. The most impressionable scene then was little Tommy Doyle getting bullied by his classmates, causing him to trip and smash the comically enormous pumpkin he's carrying. Though he just misses encountering Michael Myers, Tommy smashing his pumpkin felt more like a real-life fear to me. In first grade, I was just starting to get my first taste of what a "bully" was. I had not yet learned about masked strangers who just seemed to teleport from room to room.

The following year, CBS aired *Salem's Lot*, a two-part miniseries based on

Stephen King's novel of the same name. Still believing that it wasn't necessary to monitor what I watched, my parents let me view it with them, even though it famously featured a scene with a child vampire hovering in front of a window, a malevolent grin on his face. The child vampire stayed with me, got under my skin, far more than Michael Myers did. It triggered a lifetime of sleeping poorly, easily jostled awake by the wind rustling a tree branch against my bedroom window, my father coughing in his sleep, or sounds entirely invented by my imagination.

At the same time, I found myself intrigued by the feeling of being scared. All of my senses heightened at once made me feel smarter, more aware of my surroundings. Of course, what I really was was anxious, but I didn't know the word for that at the time. It's entirely possible that I emerged from the womb anxious, and always anticipating danger around every corner. I rarely could articulate what that danger was, so being introduced to the concept of vampires, werewolves, demons, and the like was a blessing. Some of my fears had a name, and having that information made them easier to confront. The devil you know is always better than the devil you don't, after all.

My family was an early adopter of cable television, which introduced me to an entirely new world. With absolutely no guidance from any adults in my life as to what was "appropriate viewing" or not, I dove into horror, watching everything from *The Shining* to Hammer films to straight exploitative garbage like *Humanoids From the Deep*. This fascination extended to what I read as well, and I began pilfering from my parents' book collection, which leaned heavily towards Stephen King and the pulp horror of John Saul, whose books often featured terrible things happening to children. King in particular seemed to strike a perfect balance, describing the familiar mundanities of life before some sort of unexpected monster, whether human or otherwise, tears it in half. I was already constantly on the lookout for such monsters and reading about them validated my feelings. Steve and I, we knew: they were everywhere. Under your bed. Behind a locked door. In that creepy old house. Wearing your parents' faces.

By the time my parents' marriage began to violently unravel, video rental became more widespread, and I was able to withdraw even further into horror as a refuge.

Whereas once it had been something (perhaps the only thing) my mother and I bonded over, watching old Christopher Lee Dracula movies or whatever slasher flick happened to be out together, now it was a source of conflict. I had become so withdrawn into that world that I closed most of the real world out. I had trouble speaking, and even more, trouble making friends, which was a source of great embarrassment to my mother. The obsession with horror wasn't the cause of that, of course, but rather a relief from what was the real issue: growing up in an unstable household, where it was impossible to predict if a typical day would end with me sleeping in my own bed, or being sent in my pajamas to my grandparents because my parents couldn't stop fighting with each other.

I hit adolescence around the same time they finally split up for good, and with that came a bizarre puritanical streak. In adopting an overtly straightlaced attitude, in which I would tolerate no sex talk in my presence and swore that not so much as a drop of alcohol or a puff of marijuana would pass my lips, I was pushing back against my parents' philosophy of "no boundaries" childrearing. I became the target audience for the newly created D.A.R.E., a joyless crank of a kid who would alternately look down at my peers and seethe with jealousy at the same time.

I sank deeper still into horror. Whatever rated R garbage was on cable, I'd watch it, particularly once I was living with my father, who worked nights and thus oversaw what I was doing even less than he had before. I added true crime books, an altogether new kind of horror, to my personal library. Right around this time, Stephen King published *IT*, the first-day purchase for me. I related to the bullied kids in the Losers' Club but cynically believed that I was more likely to end up gruesomely murdered by Pennywise because I spent so much time alone. Whatever friends I had in grade school had drifted away by then, having figured out the secret to surviving junior high, and weren't interested in talking about *The Beast Within* or *Fright Night* with me.

I was terribly lonely, but it was a resigned sort of loneliness. There would be times when I would make a half-hearted effort to fit in, but kids, you know, they can sniff that kind of thing out, spot a poseur from ten feet away. Trying to be cool only seemed to emphasize how uncool I was, and eventually, much to my mother's chagrin, I stopped trying. Soon, she drifted away too, treating me as though I was a mystery, she had no desire to solve.

But the movies never left me. The books never left me. Stephen King's descrip-tions of the fictitious Castle Rock sounded so like the small, work-ing-class Jersey town where I lived that it was almost comforting. I had yet to find anything else in pop culture that resembled my life and my world. I grew less fearful that monsters would get me, and more assured that we had an understanding. I believed in them, and they believed in me, and we could peacefully exist in the same space and time. More importantly, it was nice to have a secret — or at least, one I enjoyed keeping. By the time I entered high school, the 80s horror movie boom had peaked and was winding down. The first round of Satanic Panic had done its part but also it just wasn't fashionable anymore, in the same way, that Star Wars wasn't for a little while. I was equally unfashionable, so it was easy to stay loyal and not walk away from what had been there for me for so long. I was in a little country of one, a combination of Derry and Transylvania, where I could pretend, I had some say in things.

Horror fans are often accused of being gatekeepers, turning away newbies unless they've watched a prescribed list of films or are the "right" kind of horror fan. In a pre-internet world, you had to seek out people who shared your interests, so that misplaced snobbery was never really there for me. While I was resigned to being mostly alone in my love of horror, I would have gladly accepted someone into my country of one, to gush over the special effects in *The Thing* or how *Near Dark* was a cooler vampire movie than *The Lost Boys* (though *The Lost Boys* was still great, make no mistake about that.). I had never experienced the joy of watching a slasher movie at a slumber party -- the closest I had to community was other people in a movie theater or skulking around the aisles at the local video store.

Eventually, they would come. Eventually, I would find my people. It was a relief to discover that a lot of them came from the same troubled background as I did, with absent and/or abusive parents. If not, then at least they knew loneliness and isolation, and discovered a home among the monsters, finding safety in the shadows. My little country grew bigger.

So really, my parents did me a favor by leaving me to my own devices. I grew comfortable with my own company very early on. I discovered that "home" can mean many different things. I never learned to be afraid of the dark. My friends would be there.

When people ask me what the earliest movie, I remember seeing in the theater was, I don't lie anymore.

It was *Halloween*. I was six.

WHEN SURVIVAL IS ENOUGH: FINDING STRENGTH IN THE TEXAS CHAIN SAW MASSACRE

JESSICA SCOTT

Content Warning: trauma, cannibalism, violence

I don't remember much of my childhood or adolescence. It's frustrating listening to loved ones reminisce and having to tell them that I don't remember the birthday parties or vacations or other happy moments that they speak of so fondly. I don't doubt that they happened, but I don't have those same warm recollections that they've managed to hold onto. I'm glad I was able to experience them at the time, but hearing about them now without the luxury of actually remembering them feels a bit like a friend describing a wonderful party that everyone attended except for me because my invitation got lost in the mail.

After years of therapy and a few different diagnoses, including one for complex post-traumatic stress disorder (c-PTSD), I've learned that these large gaps in my memory are common for trauma survivors. My hazily recollected life makes it all the more remarkable that I have such a vivid memory of the first time I watched *The Texas Chain Saw Massacre*. I was a teenager sitting on the floor in my family's living room on a sunny afternoon—appropriate for a film that mostly takes place in malignant Texas sunlight. I was mesmerized. I felt something change that day: a shift within me, a door opening. I couldn't have told you why at the time, but Sally Hardesty's story—and the raw, unflinching way that director Tobe Hooper told it—spoke to me in a way that no other horror film ever has.

Though I loved the genre long before I saw this particular film, I always tell people that *The Texas Chain Saw Massacre* is the movie that turned me into a horror fan. It showed me the bleak, devastating heights that horror can achieve while ironically giving me hope for the future. Sally (Marilyn Burns) wasn't my first final girl, but she was the first who touched the deepest parts of me, parts I wouldn't recognize until decades later. Sally showed me that making it through trauma unscathed isn't always an option, but simply making it through at all is still something to be celebrated. Sometimes, just surviving is enough.

There is not a single moment in *The Texas Chain Saw Massacre* where the viewer feels comfortable. The sickening flashbulb sounds and cacophonous percussion crashes felt so deeply wrong, so horribly unnatural, that my stomach began to turn as soon as I hit play on that fateful sunny afternoon. However, the raw, naturalistic cinematography, with its solar flares and documentary-like graininess, let me know that this horrific unnaturalness is the most natural thing in the world. The cinéma vérité style, coupled with the repeated use of dispassionate news reports and the opening narration telling the viewer that this is a true story, force the viewer to confront the truth: the world is not safe or clean. It does not make sense. Real life is a terrifying, confusing mess of blood, tears, and unending horror. The film may not tell a factually accurate account of a real occurrence, but its heightened reality gets at a core truth that is more real than reality.

There's a dreadful inevitability to the horrific events that befall Sally and her friends. When Pam (Teri McMinn) reads Franklin (Paul A. Partain) and Sally's horoscopes, she describes the exact horrors they will soon face. The heavens are a constant focus of the film's unflinching gaze: the sun beats down on each character as if it is watching them with a malevolent eye, as voyeuristic low-angle shots emphasize this off-kilter reality where you are never free from the evil influence of the stars. This echoed my own experience growing up: trauma and tragedy are inescapable. You can fight all you want (and Sally fights like hell), but the best you can hope for is merely making it out alive.

This confirmation of our lack of safety, this sense that the world does not spin as neatly on its axis as we all like to think it does...these ideas spoke to my soul as a teenager. I was a traumatized kid who never felt safe, even at home, and I had found a film that confirmed all the unnamed feelings deep within me. Sally and Franklin visit their grandfather's old house and find macabre art littering the dilapidated rooms where they once played and slept. This signals that the deranged hitchhiker who attacked them earlier has visited their family home and brought death and desecration with him, proving that home is not a safe place. It never was. A family of depraved cannibals has been next door the whole time, and now is the time when Sally and Franklin are fated to make this horrible discovery.

Though I was transfixed by the entire film, sitting there on the floor of my own unsafe home in the middle of the day, there was one particular scene that truly changed my life. When Sally is the only remaining survivor, after witnessing the slaughter of her own brother and being tortured and mocked by the sadistic family of cannibals that have her tied up at their disgusting dinner table, she loses her final tether to the safe reality she thought she knew. Hooper alternates between ominous wide shots and discomfiting close-ups throughout the film, playing with the viewer's sense of scale to make sure they never feel comfortable or certain of this world or their relationship to it. His masterstroke, however, is in the extreme close-ups of Sally's eyes as she takes in the horror, absurdity, and visceral wrongness unfolding in front of her. The discordant score reaches a fever pitch at this point, deepening the onslaught on the viewer's senses. We can hear Sally's mind snapping as she loses her sanity while sitting at that stomach-churning dinner table; we begin to lose ours right along with her. The extreme close-ups of her desperate, searching, bloodshot eyes remind us of the solar flares arcing at the beginning of the film. Sally's veins are microcosmic sunspots, underscoring the suffocating inevitability of her horrific fate as she opens her eyes painfully wide to search for an escape that simply isn't there.

Sally never stops searching, though, and as she fights against her captors, she finds a split-second window of opportunity and takes full advantage of it. Quite literally, as she jumps through a plate glass window for the second time in the film. Sally will do anything it takes to survive, no matter how much of herself—ribbons of flesh, chunks of hair, or broken pieces of her psyche—she has to leave behind. Much of her ordeal at the cannibal homestead takes place at night, which makes it all the more shocking when she jumps out of the window and finds unexpected glaring sunlight. This startling transition adds to the sense of timelessness and unreality of Sally's trauma, which reminded me so much of my own experience. I have no sense of the past. I often lose time. Even as a teenager I knew that I wasn't whole, that I was battered and bruised like Sally Hardesty, and so her nightmare felt very familiar to me. I know what it's like to realize that home isn't the safe place it should be. I know what it's like to look at the world and see a malevolent gaze or a sheen of grime that you can never scrub off. Safety and sanity are illusions. Sally and I both learned that the hard way.

Not only is your home not a safe place; neither is your own body. When Sally is the guest of honor at the obscene dinner party, Leatherface (Gunnar Hansen) and the hitchhiker (Edwin Neal) both paw at her, fingering her hair, poking at her, and running their hands over her. Sally's body is not hers to control. She is an object to them, a piece of meat just like all the other animals (human or otherwise) that the family kills and consumes. This moment is especially difficult for me to watch, as is the moment when the hitchhiker mocks Sally for screaming and crying, pantomiming a "boohoo" motion as he laughs at her. These echo traumatic moments in my own life that make me feel as if I am crumbling from the inside out...the outside world isn't safe, but neither is my inner world. There is no refuge from the violence and horror that surrounds me.

Another lesson Sally and I both learned is that you never really stop running. After bursting through the glass into the sticky Texas sunlight, she flags down a truck driver only to watch him die at the hands of Leatherface. She then has to flag down another driver, who fortunately slows down long enough for Sally to jump into the bed of his pickup. She screams wildly at the driver to get away from the hulking psychopath still chasing her with a chainsaw. Though she speeds away from Leatherface, he's still back there, revving his chainsaw as the sun flares behind him. The scars on her mind and body will never fully heal. She will never be truly free of him, no matter how far or how fast she travels. My c-PTSD makes it feel like the trauma I experienced as a child is still happening, all around me and all the time. No matter how innocuous they are, loud noises or unexpected touches launch me into fight-flight-or-freeze mode; when you grow up never knowing when the next threat is coming, everything feels dangerous. The deep scars of the past make sure you can never truly outrun your tormentors. Even if you manage a physical escape, your brain tells you that it is only temporary, that the abuser or the chainsaw-wielding maniac is just a few steps away, waiting and watching and ready to strike.

As Sally finally escapes, she screams and cries and laughs; covered in blood and looking nearly as deranged as her tormentors, this is not the Sally viewers met at the beginning of the film. She knows now how horrifying the world actually is. She has been changed forever by her experience, and her repeated near-escapes earlier in the film have taught her that she will never be safe. The past is always coming for you, no matter how far away it feels. But you can keep running, and that's exactly what Sally does. Throughout *The Texas Chain Saw*

Massacre, Sally runs and fights and jumps through windows. She keeps going even when there seems to be no hope, even when it seems like there is no one left to trust. Bruised, slashed, violated, utterly alone, and driven mad by her ordeal at the hands of a sadistic family of cannibals, Sally Hardesty doesn't make it out in one piece, but she makes it out alive. My trauma, as it so often does, compounded. I went from traumatic home to traumatic home, entering abusive relationships without realizing what I was doing. I considered self-harm and suicide. But, just like Sally, I survived. I ran and jumped out of harmful situations and kept going even when I had no idea how to take care of myself. I'm still not entirely sure how to keep myself safe and healthy, but just like Sally, I try like hell to figure it out. Sally inspires me because she survives. She doesn't survive unscathed, but she survives. For victims of trauma, that can be enough.

The Texas Chain Saw Massacre holds the viewer's gaze and forces us to stare unblinking into the sun in order to see the truth. The world is a terrifying place, governed by malevolent forces and filled with all that is wrong, sick, and painful. That truth is something I have always known, but I didn't know how to express it until after I saw Tobe Hooper's 1974 masterpiece. Sally taught me another truth, though, and that is the importance of just making it out. I survived. I continue to survive. I may be scarred; I may be bloodied; I may be unrecognizable from who I was in a past that I can no longer remember. But I survived, and that is all that matters.

BITE-SIZED LOVE NOTES FOR SCOOBY-DOO (2002) & ITS ORIGINAL MOTION PICTURE SOUNDTRACK

DYLYN

Dedicated to mom, dad, Matthew Lillard, and the members of Mystery Inc.

As I write this at 3:30 in the morning, I have to smile at how passionate I am (zoinks! I'm even wearing my Scooby-Doo knee-highs). But with my love for this film spanning the dang ages, it's about time I give credit where credit is Doo!

So with all the little cogs in my neon green heart, I need to express why *Scooby-Doo* (2002) is not only an exceptional work of art but one of my most personal genre favorites. In fact, with three-quarters of Mystery Inc. hailing from modern horror classics (Matthew Lillard, most notably from *Scream* and *Thirteen Ghosts*, with Sarah Michelle Gellar and Freddie Prinze Jr. hailing from *I Know What You Did Last Summer*), this film is a self-referential, passionately aware chiller (not so far from *Scream* in ways) that deserves way, way, WAY more love than it gets.

As a die-hard fan of this film, however, I must also acknowledge that its soundtrack and score are equally brilliant, and my love for the music only compounds my love for the film itself. On a warm Gainesville summer night in 2002, after seeing it in theaters, my parents got me the soundtrack on CD. I swear I must have taken it everywhere. Something about the hard plastic jewel case felt so dreamy in my hands. And now that I think back on it, I believe it may have been one of the first film soundtracks I'd ever owned. As a lifelong soundtrack buff, I couldn't imagine a better start to my collection. My heart just burst every time I listened to it (which just so happened to be many times... daily), and for that reason, the best way to illustrate this film's impact on me is to take you, track by track, through this magnificent album. So without further a-Doo:

TRACK 1: SHAGGY, WHERE ARE YOU?

"Shaggy, Where Are You?" is not only the first song on the album but the first song in the film. Sung by the iconic musical artist Shaggy himself, it's a meta masterpiece that's infectiously delightful. Every time I listen to it, I'm transported back to my old room in Gainesville with the beige carpet and the wooden daybed with the heart carved on top. I have to confess I still get excited when I hear the song's opening, "Raggy? Roh!" with Lillard's Shaggy in tow ("Scooby!").

Ever since I saw him as Stu in *Scream*, I've been eternally enamored with Matthew Lillard. The emotionality he offers in his roles, how kind and compassionate he seems offscreen, his palpable enthusiasm and his commitment to his craft. With Scooby-Doo's first sequence ending with the gang's break-up, Shaggy's proclamation that "Friends don't quit" has blanketed me with warmth ever since the day I first heard it. There is, naturally, not a whole lot of realism in this film (unless you believe in anthropomorphic dogs), but I'd like to believe that such unconditional love truly does exist. As silly as it sounds, watching this film and listening to the soundtrack gives me hope that someday I'll love myself as much as I do those around me. Being a wacky, clumsy dog lover myself with my own fondness for decadent snacks, I feel close to Shaggy in many ways. But if friends really don't quit, I hope to be my own friend someday too.

TRACK 2: LAND OF A MILLION DRUMS

Outkast, Killer Mike, and Sleepy Brown's masterpiece "Land Of A Million Drums" is unparalleled in its artfulness and movement, and while it's way too hard to pick a favorite off this soundtrack, this song might take the cake in mesmerizing charm and poeticism alone. The lyrics are chock-full of references that would make any genre fan's heart soar. From a direct nod to Lillard's *Thirteen Ghosts* ("I suspect the thirteen ghosts of Scooby-Doo") to the beckoning of a late horror visionary ("Call Vincent Price up on the Nextel"), it's impossible not to feel perfectly at home in the music. Because the song plays right when the gang arrives at the film's creepy theme park, I'd like to think of it as a dedicated anthem to the island. I'd consider this to be the track that ties the entire album together, just iconic.

TRACK 3: LIL' ROMEO'S B HOUSE

Initially done by The Commodores, Romeo Miller (often known as Lil' Romeo) and Master P's version of "Brick House" is a sweet reimagining of the original. With Scooby-Doo's goofy whine throughout, the cover is bubbly, unique, and just downright good.

It makes me think back on how prevalent Romeo's music was when I was growing up. I remember being at my friend Kristen's house, hearing his Christmas song with Hilary Duff on The Disney channel— "Tell Me a Story (About the Night Before)"—and playing with my Daphne Barbie doll. Kristen used to love spraying perfume in her Barbies' hair, so I think about that too. While, of course, the early '00s were nowhere near perfect, my nostalgia goggles are especially rosy with this song.

TRACK 4: THINKING ABOUT YOU

Solange and Murphy Lee's "Thinking About You" is another tribute track, this time winking at Scooby-Doo's original theme song. While, in a large part, it stays true to the original tune, its gentler pacing and romantic twist create a beautifully sugary-sweet experience. The film, which revolves around horror and love, makes me realize how additionally influential this song has been throughout my life.

In one part, Solange sings, "Where did my baby go? Boy, take that mask off," which makes me wonder if I caught that double meaning as a child. Of course, *Scooby-Doo* is filled with disguises and masks and, in the film, literal brainwashing, but with my own perpetual awkwardness, my struggles with chronic illness, and until somewhat recently, my unspoken queerness, I've become so accustomed to my own masks that it speaks to me now on a completely different level. Additionally, her repeated line in the chorus, "...it's a mystery constantly thinking if you love me" reminds me of my own heartbreaks, ones that occur every day when I wonder where I stand with my loved ones. It seems now my own life is overflowing with mysteries too.

TRACK 5: WORDS TO ME

Unfortunately, I'm just going to have to relinquish any remaining dignity before talking about this one. I guess I'll just come out and say it: Sugar Ray's "Words To Me" and its coinciding scene in the film rule over my entire life. With its sunshiney music box intro and its candy-like but sinister lyrics, the song embraces its own sinful masks and secrets.

In the film, amidst a deadly investigation, Daphne wanders the park grounds looking for clues. Before splitting from her friends, she walks by an idyllic poolside concert led by a very possessed Sugar Ray. The two lock eyes, she gazes at him almost as if in a trance, and he sings, "I count the days 'til I see you again. You know, I tried, and I am sorry." But then, his eyes turn demon-green and his voice begins to warp, snapping Daphne right out of her love spell and back into reality. She gathers herself to not rouse suspicion, smiles politely, and Demon Ray continues, "One night can make a difference. Please don't leave me hanging on and on." And on that last blissfully melodic "on," he glowers at her menacingly and smirks at his bandmate (who does this evil little gesture with his sunglasses) as she runs away. This scene alone secures this film's place in my heart as a horror film, and if you listen closely to the lyrics, there's nothing sweet about them. If this iteration of Sugar Ray and Adam Brody's Low Shoulder collaborated, I think I'd die from pure elation, unless they stole my soul first, which is a sacrifice I am willing to make.

TRACK 6: FREAKS COME OUT AT NIGHT

Earlier, I likened *Scooby-Doo* to *Scream* with regards to their creators' killer meta consciousness, and just like the soundtracks for the Scream films, this one also contains its own top-tier covers. Uncle Kracker and Busta Rhymes' rendition of Whodini's "Freaks Come Out At Night" is yet another stellar tribute to an already brilliant song.

In the film, the song plays during a scene at an eerie bar called Dead Mike's. Within this freaky scene is Part One of one of the best jokes I've ever heard in a film. The bartender receives a call intended for Scooby and yells to the patrons, "We got a Mr. Doo here?...," to which the most classic looking stoner you can imagine (in a bright red and blue tie-dye shirt) says, "Uhhhh, Melvin Doo?" And I suppose this isn't knee-slapping territory by itself, but near the end, when

Scooby is about to be sacrificed, there's a callback to the joke when Scooby throws this poor guy under the bus, saying "Don't you mean Melvin Doo?" It's plain and simple cinematic perfection. But it also makes me think of my first dog and late best friend Melvin who watched this film with me a million times over.

TRACK 7: BUMP IN THE NIGHT

Allstars' "Bump in The Night" feels just like a Halloween party to me. It so magnificently captures the essence of the family-friendly haunts you'd see in productions like this or in other gentle horrors like the original cartoon *Halloweentown, Goosebumps, So Weird,* or *Are You Afraid of the Dark?* Even more, I think this is one of the first songs I used to teach myself how to sing (and I'm a sucker for the creaky door sound effect at the end as well). I think I miss being allowed to be unabashedly ridiculous, or at least, I miss some of the vibrant shmaltziness encapsulated in that era.

TRACK 8: WHENEVER YOU FEEL LIKE IT

I'll preface this by saying that there are no bad songs on the album. In fact, each song is incomparably breathtaking. Having said that, I've come to appreciate Kylie Minogue's "Whenever You Feel Like It" much more now than I did as a child. As another one of the slower-paced tracks on the soundtrack—like "Thinking About You"—the whispered romance of it all is something I had to first experience to understand. Even so, the song has always made me think of angelic ballet dances and flowy ghostlike clothing. Plus, I'll forever have a soft spot for "You're a devil, you're a rebel, that's why I need you, baby."

TRACK 9: IT'S A MYSTERY

Speaking of romance, Little T and One Track Mike's "It's A Mystery" is quite possibly the most romantic song I've ever heard. Played in a scene where Shaggy wins a crane machine prize for his new love Mary Jane (played by the eternally precious Isla Fisher), there's a vulnerable honesty within that song that perfectly complements Mary Jane's "Nobody's ever given me a stuffed dismembered head before" line. If I'm being vulnerable now myself, this song speaks to me so loudly that I usually tear up or cry when I listen to it. Within the lyrics, the boy goes on a date with his crush who so clearly adores him back, but he cannot make heads or tails of why she likes him.

During the song, their date is explained through a series of misadventures and clever jokes, but the imperfections of any true human connection, certainly the one described in this song, are often what makes them so real and beautiful. Even as I write that now, I still acknowledge I'm just as perplexed when someone shows me that they care for me. "You told me in a whisper so quiet that we could go steady if I was down to try it. Right then, I should have known you were serious, but even now your love is mysterious."

TRACK 10: SCOOBY D

Is there anything the Baha Men can't do? No. Absolutely not! Their song "Scooby D," just like any of their other songs, is an absolute treasure. It breaks my heart that we don't hear much about this band anymore. They used to pop up constantly in films, and their popular hit "Who Let the Dogs Out?" was a staple of many peoples' childhoods. This particular track has a haunting ghoul-like voice throughout and also features some joyously lyrical woofs, perhaps an intentional reference to their other music or, maybe, just a perfect coincidence.

TRACK 11: MAN WITH THE HEX

The Atomic Fireballs' "Man With The Hex" is one of the faster-paced songs on the album, even coming up during one of the greatest action sequences in the whole film. In this high-intensity scene, all of the island's creepy secrets are beginning to unravel and reveal themselves. "Man With The Hex" plays while ghastly purple demons chase the park-goers, Scooby almost dies from getting distracted by a sandwich (a common occurrence for both him and myself alike), Scooby and the gang crash through a glass window, and the film descends into its signature cartoony chaos.

TRACK 12: GROW UP

Something about "Grow Up" and Simple Plan's viscerally rebellious brat-titude has become a crucial source of empowerment for me as an adult. As a kid, belting this in my room made me feel so edgy and cool. I was (am) a shy little only child, and I was raised with lots of love but also lots of rules: Hebrew school every Sunday, early curfews, no dyed hair. Since then, I've struggled to release much of my boring goody-good proclivities. I look to songs like this to keep my feral side intact, and while the lyrics are admittedly, viciously funny, I believe they were intended to be that way. But, honestly, it just goes to show that goofiness is great no matter what age you are. I seriously hate the capitalist notion that fun should only play a small part, if any, in our lives. In a perfect world, I think we'd all be relentlessly encouraged to "...stay up late, spend hours on the phone" and "hang out with our friends to our hearts content."

TRACK 13: SCOOBY-DOO, WHERE ARE YOU?

I'm ashamed to admit this, but after 75 years of listening to this soundtrack religiously, it had to be pointed out to me that Simple Plan's "Grow Up" referenced MxPx right before MxPx's actual track on the album ("GC, Sum and Blink and MxPx rocking my room"). Either way, MxPx's cover of Scooby-Doo, Where Are You?'s theme song is the closest to a straight cover on the soundtrack. Preserving most of the foundations of the original song, they cover the theme in their standard pop-punk style, creating a monstrously cute dialogue with Simple Plan and the track that played before this. Ultimately, being the last song with vocals on the album, this high energy theme song serves as a graceful transition to the final track: a short but exciting medley of the score.

TRACK 14: MYSTERY INC.
(AND MY OWN FINAL THOUGHTS)

Composer David Newman's "Mystery Inc." is the last track on the album and, simultaneously, a powerfully condensed look into the film's score. Like the film itself, this shortened version of the score is an emotional ride. It's especially intense, however, because they jammed almost two hours of music into about only three and a half minutes. This isn't a complaint though, because I'm in love with this song, and listening to it gives me flutters like I'm being held.

Track 14 brings me back to my bedroom with the beige carpet, back to my old boombox, dolls and stuffed animals—Reindeer, Aurora, and Rosebud— back to my mom baking challah in the kitchen and my dad building or fixing something. It makes me think of the gang's breakup; how they all left even after Shaggy said, "Please don't go." It makes me think about how they subsequently ended up back together because that kind of love is totally possible amongst people (and dogs) who care for each other. It makes me think about how many times I've quit on myself and what Shaggy said about every member of Mystery Inc. being supremely important for different reasons.

In the scene at Dead Mike's, Shaggy tells Mary Jane that Fred called his crane machine skill "a worthless talent." Instead of taking that to heart though, he uses his skill to win her a cute little plush all while maintaining his wonderfully zany self. In the background, Little T and One Track Mike's song plays, but if you check out the full song on the album, you hear, "It's a mystery why a girl like you would want a boy like me." After nearly two decades of obsessing over this film and soundtrack, I'm starting to realize that my loved ones care about me because of my own wonderful zaniness. As Shaggy says early on, "...we all play an important part in this group." And "like a big, delicious banana split," every single ingredient is vital.

NOTHING SO APPALLING: WORDS OF LOVE FOR THE BIZARRE AND BEAUTIFUL FRINGES OF HORROR FILMS

JACK VAN TUYLE

A well-executed horror film forces its audience to grapple with the inevitability of death and the cruel absurdity of suffering. It's what a horror fan craves. And yet, today, I'd like to encourage you to take a moment to explore films that, instead, might make you laugh or groan. Today I'm here to discuss the movies I truly love. The trash. The filth. The sleaze. The real low-down-low-budget-never-Oscar-nominated funky junk. In this era of prestige horror cinema, films like *Get Out* and *Hereditary* are executing at a standard of excellence comparable to classics like *The Exorcist* and John Carpenter's *Halloween*. These are movies I find shocking, harrowing, even life-changing. But, while so many others are already celebrating these films' mainstream success, let's take a moment to revel in the uniquely queer joy to be found in B-movie horror.

While the horror genre by no means corners the market on trashy movies (and any glance at the Hallmark Channel during the winter holidays will prove this), it is remarkable for its distinct and particular odors of trash. There's just something ineffable about these kinds of lurid, dirty horror movies, particularly those from the 1950s to the 1990s. Sure, you could say that movies like *The Cabinet of Dr. Caligiri* are more enriching than movies like *Pieces*. And maybe you'd be right. I would respond, however, by asking: where else will I see a human being chopped to bits with a chainsaw just after pissing themselves? Where else will I see a creature made of reanimated human remains, with perfectly manicured stiletto nails, rip the protagonist's genitals off just as the end credits begin to roll? Sure, many other movies have the "good sense" to decline to show us something so salacious, but *Pieces* drags good taste into the trashcan and shows scenes that have some in the audience retching while others split their sides with laughter. Isn't that kind of wonderful?

What makes these movies so enthralling, for me, is that they are capable of obliterating our hegemonic, quotidian standards of filmmaking, and in so doing present audiences with something that is truly alternative in its twisted revelry. For example, I present the whacked-out exploitation film *Blood Freak*. Starring D-List actor Steve Hawkes as a hunky biker torn between a half-hearted love for Jesus and a burgeoning pot addiction, Blood Freak was co-directed, co-produced, and co-written by Hawkes (alongside Brad F. Grinter of *Flesh Feast*) after a botched fire effect on the set of *Tarzán y el arco iris* burned over 90 percent of his body, leaving him up to his eyeballs in medical debt and stranded in Florida. *Blood Freak* is described on the back of its box (for the *Something Weird Video* DVD release) as "the world's only Turkey-Monster-Anti-Drug-Pro-Jesus-Gore film!". You may be asking, "how does this movie use gratuitous shlock and violence to spread a Christian message??" The answer is: unsuccessfully. The acting in *Blood Freak* is detached from human behavior on a basic level, and the mise-en-scene hovers between uncomfortably grimey and hilariously kitsch; but the poor choices and lack of taste, for me, make for an extremely welcoming atmosphere. The threadbare dialogue is just free space for my friends and I to shout out our own ideas and perverse interpretation. Every failed special effect reminds us that, yes, even untrained weirdos like us can make a movie. There are lots of ways to describe *Blood Freak* that are far from charitable, but believe me, you will never forget seeing a part turkey part man-monster cut off a drug dealer's leg with a table saw and drink the blood shooting from the stump. And if this ragtag group of desperate creators can make that happen, there's hope for all of us.

Blood Freak was only one of many films that pushed exploitation films to absurd and delightful limits. Often these films were made by directors like Herschell Gordon Lewis, Andy Milligan, Doris Wishman, and Ted V. Mikels, among others. Although prolific and often successful as commercial filmmakers, these directors, and many others like them, have been widely left out of film studies discourse. To quote Paul Watson in his essay 'There's No Accounting for Taste: Exploitation Cinema and the Limits of Film Theory.' "From its first moments Film Studies' theories and canons have been bound up with an economy of taste which influences questions not only of how to approach cinema, but questions of what cinema to approach in the first instance," he continues, "This is not to say that there haven't been shifts in the cinematic canon, or that those canons are uncontested, but that those shifts and contests are themselves tied to shifts in taste which have tended overwhelmingly to exclude exploitation."(68). As a queer person then, I find the very marginality of these films relatable and inspiring. These directors may not have had the team, tools, training, or talent necessary to make a conventionally good film, but they made films anyway. They survived where they were encouraged not to. And, while these directors have been widely ignored within the subject of film studies, as time has gone on they have earned reputations among freak film seekers as a particular strain of outsider artists, each of them with their own distinct style and voice. It's truly gratifying to see these weird films live on.

Among these outsider filmmakers, no name looms larger than that of the notorious, the infamous, the fabulous Edward D. Wood Jr. Wood began his career with the trans-sexploitation film *Glen Or Glenda*, a boldly confessional auteur effort that cemented Wood's place as a queer maverick filmmaker and a true pioneer at the edges of acceptability. Wood's career spanned from the '50s to the '70s, and throughout that time he worked with horror icons Bela Lugosi and Vampira and helped to make a star out of Tor Johnson. Many say Ed Wood was an awful director. Maybe even "The Worst of All Time" (Medved). People say the way Ed Wood writes and directs a story lacks any good sense or taste, and, truthfully, his films were exclusively bottom of the barrel, dirt cheap productions. Personally, I love Ed Wood. In fact, he may be one of my very favorite figures in the history of film. Ed Wood films do what all my favorite horror stories do, they are unafraid to go to the edge of what is expected, no matter how deeply, profoundly bizarre that may appear. From those recesses of the mind, Ed Wood fearlessly and shamelessly pulls stories that reflect a unique vision. Ed Wood represents, perhaps better than any other filmmaker, what cultural critic Jack Halberstram calls "The Queer Art Of Failure", which Halberstram describes as ". . . the refusal of legibility, and an art of unbecoming . . .drama without a script, narrative without progress." Halberstram continues, saying: "The queer art of failure turns on the impossible, the improbable, the unlikely, and the unremarkable. It quietly loses, and in losing it imagines other goals for life, for love, for art, and for being." I believe that Ed Wood's 'failure' according to the conventional standards makes way for new possibilities in storytelling. It allowed him to do what no other director could. In the introduction to their screenplay for the biopic *Ed Wood*, screenwriters Scott Alexander and Larry Karaszuewski said, ". . . Ed didn't actually produce usable exploitation. His Films were less concerned with entertainment value than with getting his obsessions on the screen. Angora, dead bodies, space monsters, old cowboy actors, pleas for universal tolerance, stock footage. . .". This illustrates perfectly how Wood's failures as a conventional filmmaker allowed him to express himself fully in new, wholly independent ways. Furthermore, what is often seen as a lack of technique and craftsmanship on Wood's part could be interpreted as an inventiveness of technique. The dream sequence in *Glen or Glenda*, I feel, is a particular example of this. Through bare and off-kilter sets, non-sequitur editing, and imagery of sadomasochistic sexual acts, Wood makes, on the cheap, one of the best depictions of the fear that comes from living a "closeted" life. The pain of wanting so badly to be understood, and to be seen, pitted against the terror of being rejected, and the paranoia of seeing yourself as corrupt or immoral because of your own queerness. It is almost surrealist filmmaking. And, while *Glen or Glenda* is not a horror picture, the nightmarish imagery throughout this sequence of devils, accusatory mobs, and an eerie performance by Bela Lugosi certainly do more than a little to evoke a sense of the horrifying.

Wood would expand this blend of sexploitation and horror when he wrote the screenplay for one of his most famous pictures: *Orgy of The Dead*, an absurd wonder of a movie. It's one part unchoreographed topless dancing, one part uncontrollable fog machine, topped off with a cast of Universal Monster characters creeping around the edges of the very limited "set". And the wigs are extraordinary. After watching the dancers, each of whom performs a directionless set for about three solid minutes, the sex appeal of the nudity falls completely flat, and each scene becomes at first laughable and then admirable. After all, it's brave of these performers to leave their ordinary lives behind to participate in something so bizarre and so obviously ill-conceived. I, for one, can't help but look gleefully at the way *Orgy of The Dead* blends the most base impulses of the nudie cutie genre with a warped approach to recreating the mood and mystery of classic Universal Monster films. It's shameless, like all good sleaze (make no mistake Ed Wood is sleazy) and in that shamelessness, I see a dedication to telling stories and sharing ideas that make me want to make art. Filthy horror movies like Ed Wood's are inspiring to me in a way few other films are. Ed Wood's movies can be laughable, yes. They can be absurd, absolutely. But even so, Wood was undeniably a trailblazer for queer filmmaking and independent filmmaking in general.

When I recommend these kinds of "trashy" or "campy" horror movies to people, I have often gotten replies like, "oh, there's so many movies out there

I could be watching instead. Why would I waste my time watching something like this?" Although I never see these movies as a waste of time, I can see where this line of thinking comes from. Film, like any art form, has its own discipline after all, and this discipline is, at this point, well understood. Throughout the course of more than a century, filmmakers and audiences have become accustomed to certain formal techniques. With that comes certain expectations for how a film ought to be assembled. When these expectations of execution are met, when the film is well-acted, well written, well-edited, etc., we call these "good movies." Why watch a movie that's "bad" when there are so many movies which work so hard to be "good"? I do not believe that artists, advertisers, and worldwide audiences are wrong to uphold techniques that reliably convey meaning and inspire emotion. Rather, I would just like to say that the discipline of filmmaking is just that: a discipline. To quote Halberstram again, "Disciplines qualify and disqualify, legitimate and delegitimate, reward and punish; most important, they statically reproduce themselves and inhibit dissent." Films that do not meet up to the standards set by the discipline of filmmaking are disregarded. Horror has always had a reputation as an outsider genre. I believe that the very thing that makes horror so engrossing as a genre is exactly what gives it its "outsider" reputation. Horror films engage with their audience not by fulfilling audience expectations but by upsetting those expectations. I believe that trashy horror movies, sleazy horror movies, with their idiosyncrasies and unorthodox techniques, can be doubly effective at giving audiences a completely unique experience.

A term that I've often heard used to describe some of the movies I've discussed here is "So bad it's good." I've always preferred to think about these movies as "so different, they're good." We have so many movies that have told the same story endlessly. Especially now, with media conglomerates expanding their empire of intellectual properties at a worrying rate, theaters closing, and more and more remakes being made, it seems like finding something really original is harder than ever before. But the weird B-movie treasure is out there, and these movies can completely rewire your brain. They are quietly revolutionary, in that they open you up to a whole world of film where you can leave behind their rigid perspective on "good" or "bad" art. And, if you allow yourself to leave those notions behind, you will uncover wilder and further possibilities in art, even when those possibilities are deeply, deeply strange. It gives me a vision of a creative future for myself and other weirdos and what we might be able to do with some cameras, cheap wigs, and a few gallons of fake blood.

"Seldom can it be said of a Motion Picture that it stands alone. One of a kind. A motion picture that jars you, rocks you, astonishes you beyond the point of endurance! A Taste Of Blood is such a motion picture ..."
-From the trailer for Herschell Gordon Lewis' *A Taste Of Blood*

HORROR GAVE ME BACK MY LAUGH

CATHERINE E. BENSTEAD

As a child I was strictly business: there was no way in hell you would have caught me laughing at my own mistakes or misfortune. I had managed to develop unrelenting standards for myself, and one of those standards was that life was serious, and there was no room for funny business. Not once would you catch my mouth even remotely resembling a smirk if I had hurt myself in a comedy of errors. Catherine E. Benstead was as deadpan as Wednesday Addams, with self-criticism slicing through her confidence like a butcher's knife. Now that is not to say that I didn't know how to laugh; my father has always told me I have a wicked sense of humour. Laughing was normal and part of growing up with my younger sister and our hilarious Dad, who has not only a great sense of humour but a quick wit and can tell stories that captivate an entire room.

Every time someone dared to laugh at me, hours of agonising rumination from the sheer embarrassment would ensue. As a hypersensitive kid, having someone laugh at me meant that I had made a mistake: I had screwed up, or I was being rejected as abnormal or weird. Growing up I spent a lot of time with my sister and my male cousins, as there weren't many girls on my dad's side of the family. All rough and tough boys made growing up a little harder than it should have been. When I was nine years old, I knocked out my younger cousin's front tooth. While my sister and older cousin spent hours laughing at the situation, I spent hours ruminating in my bedroom. I was terrified of what my aunt, nan, dad, uncle, mother, anyone who learned about the situation was going to say about me or to me. I don't particularly remember the outcome of the amateur tooth removal I had performed on my cousin; I don't think I even got more than a "try not to be silly, be safer" lecture. On the inside, I was caving in. I had hurt someone. I had fucked up. I was worthless.

This feeling of worthlessness carried on throughout my teenage years. It meant that I had this innate need to grab life by the throat and ring all the opportunities out of it I could get to prove that I was a heavyweight contender. Throughout high school, I was an overachiever, a performing arts student, taking on every extracurricular music activity I could. When it came to crunch time I flopped; exams were a horrifying experience, and my anxiety caused me to flake on even attempting to study. I managed to get into university, and it took me five years to graduate with a Bachelor of Social Science. Throughout my first years of university, I pushed myself. I pushed myself so hard that the pressure caused me to collapse, and I fell into alcohol, drugs, and not achieving anything at all. For years I grappled with the inability to laugh at life's curve balls because that would mean I had failed at something. Laughing at myself was the most critical activity I could do against myself, and it was the ultimate betrayal. There is a concept within the neurodivergent community of masking. I constantly wore a mask of perfection and high standards; behind that mask, I was struggling to keep on track. Every day I put on that mask, made sure that I wasn't making mistakes, and making sure that the mask didn't slip and show people that I wasn't perfect.

It wasn't until my early twenties that I was introduced to horror comedy as a genre, and I rapidly fell in love with the idea. I had never realised that horror movies could be funny, yet there I was watching *Shaun of The Dead*, laughing until I cried, and my sides hurt. A dichotomy exists when it comes to horror. We know that horror is associated with the dark and morbid while in contrast humour is on the other end of the spectrum with light and humility. Therefore, it seems astounding that the two could come together and achieve the same stimulus. There I stood enthralled by the two concepts coming together to show me the non-serious side of horror. It is with this concept in mind that I can understand that horror, in general, has taught me to laugh my way through life. Comedy elements are present throughout some of our most beloved horror films, including *A Nightmare on Elm Street* (1985), *Scream* (1994), *Jennifer's Body* (2009), and *Carrie* (1978). Each one shows us elements of either ourselves or society that we find humorous. Whether it's sarcasm, slapstick, or even social commentaries that enlighten us, they all can be funny. Whilst watching horror movies, I had a realisation that life is to be enjoyed and not taken to the lengths of seriousness that I did. Horror movies have been like breathing oxygen from another source that is providing me with nutrients like laughter, self-awareness, and humility for myself and others. It's been a transformational process. When reflecting on the transformation that I have made throughout my early to late twenties, I see where my sense of humour has developed.

Over the years my humour (with the influence of my sister and Dad) has taken a dark turn, morbid even, but I don't think that necessarily makes me a bad person. In fact, I think it makes me an even more empathetic and compassionate one. One of my absolute favourite movies is *Drag Me to Hell* (2009) by Sam Raimi. Christine Brown, a loans officer, finds herself dragged through the most ridiculous situations. The dark comedy and gross gags that are placed throughout the film helped me to explore schadenfreude as a completely normal human emotion. Instead of laughing because Christine deserves the misfortune, we laugh because she is the unluckiest person on the face of the planet. We've all been there, right? My Grandma always taught me that bad things come in lots of threes: stub a toe, catch a cold, your car gets a flat tire, those are three "bad things." However, in this film, Christine hits her three bad things, and the misfortune continues, escalating into hilarious situations that normally wouldn't be that funny (or relatable) without the touch of Sam Raimi. The joy of schadenfreude was probably one of the first steps I took towards discarding the unrelenting standards I had created for myself. Discarding self-criticism and moving towards self-acceptance as a flawed human was incredibly difficult and frustrating. Now I not only find moments of joy in others' misfortune (within reason —I am not a sadist), but I have been able to seek shelter in the contentment with my own. The Japanese have a saying that goes "the misfortune of others tastes like honey," and my journey towards self-acceptance was tasting sweeter by the day.

Whilst schadenfreude has become one of the elements attributed to the darker side of my sense of humour, I have found a sense of peace when I witness horror movies with characters who have the same sense of humour as adult me. At the end of 2020, I watched Steven Kostanski's *Psycho Goreman* (2020), and I have never laughed so hard at a character so dark and deranged as Mimi. This young girl reminded me of the girl I wanted to be when I was younger, with her dark sensibilities, her quick wit, and her ability to say "frig off" to anything that got in her way. Mimi was the child I was underneath it all, the kid who didn't give a frig and went with the flow (whilst also being borderline psychopathic —like most kids, right?). When I was younger, I wanted to be like that so painfully bad. I can sit and laugh at how incredible of a character she is because, even though I couldn't be her, I knew I had the potential to be. I would have killed to have been able to tell my monsters to get out of here with the same strength and candidness. Reflecting on the hardness of my character as a child and then as a young adult, I have been able to accept that I wasn't a particularly funny child or even a soft one at that. However, as an adult, I have developed a deep respect for the person I have become and where I have come from. It's a little ironic when you think about it, not turning out the way you had planned as a child, although this path isn't so bad.

One thing that I have learned about irony is that humour lies in incongruity when it comes to what someone does and what someone says. I've always reveled in the way in which a filmmaker can create the most perfect ironic moment amidst the cataclysm of a life-changing event. In the ending of *The Cabin in the Woods,* we see our protagonists Dana (the virgin) and Marty (the stoner) face the end of the world with the most resignation someone can have in that situation. Despite the fact that they had spent the entire movie attempting to stay alive and to stop the end of the world, and with complete imperturbation, they accept the things they cannot prevent. For me, I think the humour lies in the cliche saying, "help me to accept the things that I cannot change." It might be dark that they are waiting for the end of time, but to me, there lies a much deeper meaning. Why not when facing darkness, can we not revel in humour? Why can't we spark up a joint when it feels like our world is coming down on us? It's part of my own development that has taken some time to come to terms with: there is absolutely nothing wrong with accepting that things can't go another way at that point. So why not embrace it? For someone like myself, controlling every aspect of life's curveballs was a pastime, but now I embrace them and light up my metaphoric joint whilst I watch the chaos, usually with a smile on my face.

The ability to be able to laugh at myself, embrace the uncertainty of life, and shed the stress and pressure I had put on myself was a transforming moment. The "serious business" Cat I had created seemed to have existed almost a lifetime ago, and I can still remember the first moments as the new Cat broke through my hardened shell. As I have grown into an older thirty-something-year-old woman who constantly laughs at the ebbs and flows of the world and misfortunes around me, I can look back at the hypercritical self that I have managed to shed (although sometimes she lurks in the dark). Horror movies have created a world for me where flawed protagonists take on monsters, the dark, and evil with hilarity, humility, and uncertainty. It's a world that has shown me that we are allowed to laugh at ourselves. We are funny, we are flawed, and we are human.

ISOLATION, NEURODIVERSITY AND THE STORY OF HOW HORROR SAVED MY LIFE

E.L. KING

Content Warning: sexual abuse of a minor

"Normal is an illusion. What is normal for the spider is chaos for the fly."
- Charles Addams

For as long as I can remember, I've been an observer. An outsider looking in on the stories of others. Trying to make sense of the world and why I felt like an emotional jigsaw that never quite fit. A lot of factors contributed to these feelings. The story of how horror saved me begins in a very dark place. To tell it properly, I'm going to have to cut open scabbed over wounds that likely won't ever heal. At the end of the journey, you'll understand why an isolated, neurodivergent, non-binary femme craves horror and uses it to connect with the world.

It wasn't until grade school that I understood that I was different from other kids. I was neurodivergent and couldn't keep up with the others. I wasn't learning like they were or expressing myself socially like they were. Eventually, they discovered that I'm dyslexic. I suffer from Double Deficit Dyslexia which means I struggle with both phonological processing and rapid naming. As an added quirk, my neurodivergence comes with hypersensitivity to touch or the sensation of things touching my skin. I am also prone to outbursts and at times unable to regulate my emotional responses to stimuli, especially negative stimuli brought on by anxiety or stress.

The school I attended put me in the special education classes and while I was too high functioning to remain in those classes, I couldn't read due to dyslexia. I underwent special therapy and recall having to do hours of sessions that focused on my vision response, auditory response and I even learned how to hold a pencil a special way so I could write. You could probably call me a Hooked on

Phonics success story because I had to do that too. While my symptoms have improved much since the ages of five to eight, I did develop a slight speech impediment and still struggle with my dyslexia.

However, what added to my difficulties as a child was the real-life horror story unfolding for me. I was experiencing sexual abuse at the hands of a man seventy years my senior while in his care. He wasn't even a family friend. Just the stepfather of a man my mother was dating. I pushed the events down into a dark place so they couldn't hurt me, but I have vivid flashbacks of what happened to me and nightmares to this day. Unbeknownst to me, I had post-traumatic stress disorder that went untreated until I was in my thirties. At that time, I was prone to self-harm episodes, comforting myself with food and contemplating ending my life during my darkest depression after experiencing a similar trauma as an adult. My mother blames herself and won't talk about what happened to me as a child, but denial doesn't work for me. The remaining evidence of what he did is a patch of my hair that went prematurely grey from the trauma, so I'm reminded of what happened every time my hair grows out. I cover it with dye and see a therapist nowadays, but the pain still feels like a heavy weight on my chest more than 30-years later.

I remember the smell of cigarettes hanging in the air, Virginia Slims, that's what my grandmother chain-smoked from her brown armchair, the sweetness of menthols still reminds me of her. I remember I used to craft dollhouses out of the empty boxes when I didn't have any toys to play with. I was living with my mother and brother in a small yellow flower pattern wallpapered room in the back of her double-wide trailer because we'd run out of money. As children, we were often left alone to our own devices and I found myself raising my younger brother, despite being a child myself while my Mother wasn't home. Our parents divorced several years earlier, and I only have flashback memories of this time period in my life.

Most of my childhood is a blank space, like a corrupted file locked away in my mind. The memories have been suppressed to protect me from the traumatic events that transpired and can't be accessed in a normal state of consciousness. When I was scared, feeling overwhelmed or like I might implode, I'd hide under my Grandmother's bed and soothe myself by running the blue stringy carpet through my fingers. It was one of the few sensations against my skin that didn't trigger my hypersensitivity to touch. It was just me and her hidden bottle of triple-distilled Canadian Mist whisky under there, but I hid both literally and figuratively, isolating myself early on to protect myself from the children that teased me and the boogeymen that hurt children behind locked doors.

One day my grandmother found me hiding under the bed and coaxed me out into her tiny living area with its wood-paneled walls and crocheted doilies on every surface to watch a horror film with her. My Grandmother was a creature of habit. She'd sit in her chair with her remote, a black Bic pen and the TV Guide underlining everything she planned to watch. I settled in to watch the movie she'd selected just in front of my grandmother's legs as she ran her fingers through my hair to soothe me. Her hands were soft, wrinkled and cold against my skin.

That day, we watched Stephen King's *Silver Bullet* (1985) starring Corey Haim. The film had been adapted from King's novella Cycle of the Werewolf published in 1983 and he'd written the script. This was my introduction to King long before I could comprehend what a master of horror was. I'd never before fathomed a creature as fantastical as a werewolf. I'd heard about wolves that ate grandmothers and children in books like *Little Red Riding Hood* but knew that those stories were just fairy tales. To this day, *Silver Bullet* is one of my favorite horror films. It follows Marty Coslaw, a wheelchair-bound boy who encounters a monster by the lake on the Fourth of July in his small town of Tarker's Mill, Maine. Having uncovered the identity of the creature he believes to be a werewolf, Marty, his sister Jane played by Megan Follows and Uncle Red played by Gary Busey are faced with having to defeat the monster by forging a single silver bullet and lying in wait for the next full moon. The werewolf reversion scene coordinated by Jeff Jarvis and the special effects makeup by artist Michael McCraken still captivates me. In my opinion, it's one of the best werewolf transformation scenes in horror film history, but it's rarely credited as such due to other werewolf-centric horror film releases of the same decade.

Reflecting on my first horror film experience, I know that although I couldn't articulate it at the time, I identified with Marty. His feelings of isolation at not being as able-bodied as the other kids and his overall otherness, I could see in myself. Finding that I could escape my reality by immersing myself in a horror film like Silver Bullet where a child can stand up to and defeat a grown man or a monster brought me solace. While I couldn't confront the ghoul that haunted my childhood and stalked my nightmares, I could cope with my trauma in some small way through horror films. That's the first time that horror saved my life. Being so young, I couldn't externalize the anguish I felt beyond acting out with the occasional tantrum. Instead, I often shut down completely, became introverted and barely spoke. This early experience with horror is why I find myself so passionate about the genre and always hungry to learn more about not only horror films but all horror mediums and horror theory.

Horror films can help us to cope with real-life trauma and for me, they remain an invaluable coping tool. The effect you get from watching a horror film is a primary tenet of what's called exposure therapy, forcing us to face fear as a way to overcome it. I don't find it odd that watching horror is a comforting experience. As a survivor and someone who has experienced trauma, I think I understand it better than most. We watch and crave horror for different reasons. It's the relevance and escapism that I seek for myself. Horror brings me comfort when the dark realities of life feel like they might crush me. Traumatic experiences don't leave you. They are like a blade that dulls over time with each new real-life horror acting as a sharpener to reopen old wounds. You can't truly understand the horror of trauma unless you've lived it. It's not an understanding I'd wish on anyone.

My passion for the genre in all of its forms has manifested into a podcast and indie publishing project that helps me to focus my energy and connect with people. Horror not only provides me with a way to cope with my post-traumatic stress disorder, but it has given me a creative outlet. I've always struggled with human connection and horror has created a bridge for me to a support system and community that I didn't have growing up. I'm still neurodivergent, but I don't feel so isolated as I once did. I've found a home in horror; a place to finally belong. That's why I've come to identify myself as a phobophile that will always hunger for horror.

ON MENTAL HEALTH, CREATION, AND HORROR

HARI BERROW

Content Warning: Mental Illness, abusive relationships, alcohol, drugs, and death

Darkness. The near-silence of swaying trees. You sit on the floor in your room, comfortable cushion under your bum, back lengthened but not overly tight, eyes closed, and you breathe. A little voice murmurs from your phone, reminding you to come back to the present moment, to focus on the physical sensations, to measure your in-breath and your out-breath. Stillness. Ease. For a moment, you are calm.

A sharp noise. A high-pitched squeak. A burrowing sensation. You feel a beetle crawling underneath your skin, up your cheek and towards your temple. You let out a small shriek, grab your face, try to knock off whatever is wriggling underneath your skin.

You look in your hand, check the mirror. There's nothing there. No insect. No marks. No anomalies on your face. You're just there, on your floor, with your comfortable cushion under your bum.

You breathe, try to calm yourself down, try to tell yourself it must have been a trapped nerve or a muscle spasm. You close your eyes, settle yourself on your cushion, lengthen your back, and try again.

The squeak comes back. The burrowing comes back. The crawling under your skin comes back. It comes back every time you try to practice mindfulness, and it happens for months and months and months.

At any given point, around 10% of the global population will be suffering from a recorded mental health disorder (GBD, 2017, pg.1839). This figure does not include people who do not have adequate access to healthcare; people who do not qualify for a mental health diagnosis; people who refuse a mental health diagnosis; people who do not know how to access mental health support; or people who do not want to access mental health support. In short, that figure is a conservative estimate. Whatever the prevalence of mental health conditions wherever you are, difficulties with mental health are a fact of life, and they affect more of us than we would generally think.

In early 2019, I had to come to terms with the fact that I was battling with post-traumatic stress as the result of an abusive relationship, coupled with the particularly distressing loss of my father to cancer. I had been dealing with post-traumatic stress for around two years. I had been an actor and had recently started a Master's in Creative Writing, specialising in scripts and creative nonfiction. In 2018, I had been quite lucky and been given a generous number of opportunities to work onstage. As the year progressed, however, I'd found rehearsing and performing increasingly unpleasant. The stress had become less and less manageable, and what had been excitement in previous years had turned to what was on good days unbearable anxiety, and on bad days complete, uninterested numbness. It was becoming increasingly worrying for my family, and my fizzy neural wiring had already decimated what had been the best relationship I have ever been in.

I'm not telling you this to make you feel sorry for me. I'm not telling you this to upset you. As I'm writing this to you now, I am undertaking a PhD in Creative and Critical Writing exploring how writers might represent mental health issues in scripted work. I'm a professional scriptwriter, I'm back in the best relationship I have ever been in, and I have been in recovery for around two years. I'm explaining this to you because I would like you to understand that I understand at least some of the lived experiences that come with mental ill-health. I'm also trying to write a story that will keep you interested when we get to some of the more technical sections of this essay.

You go to the cinema with a friend to watch a film about a cult. Onscreen, a young blonde woman is mourning the loss of her family. She is trying to manage the pain and the grief, trying to keep herself from spilling over, but the hurt is dizzying, and it comes out over and over and over again.

The film is shocking, violent, and disturbing, and finally, something does reach inside of you—something does make you feel—but it isn't the shock or the violence or the disturbance. This grief, and the shame that goes with it, is something you have felt over and over and over again, and your tears fall too; uncontrollable, heavy, and raw. Recently, you've wanted to watch more and more horror films. They're the only things that can keep your attention. You watch them avidly, hoping to find something that disturbs you, that frightens you, that reaches down and touches something inside you and jolts you out of the numbness that's slowly pulling the neurons apart in your head.

I'm sure that I am not the only person in this anthology to discuss the impact that Ari Aster's *Midsommar* (2019) has had on their work. For me, the release of *Midsommar* represented a turning point in both my writing and my academic life – I would not be the scriptwriter I am without having seen *Midsommar*, and I would not be doing my PhD without the release of *Midsommar*. What I saw when I went to the cinema that day was myself reflected back at me. Feelings of grief, trauma, and displacement that I had never seen in anyone else that I knew, that I had always felt were a symptom of my own weakness, were shown in vivid pastel pinks and blues, and—for the first time in four years—I felt like I wasn't alone. I am not alone in feeling this way: articles stating that *Midsommar* is 'one of the most cathartic films ever made' (Ryan, 2019), and others suggesting that certain scenes are 'indescribably cathartic to watch' (Lane, 2019) are in abundance, and reflect the thousands of individuals who felt acknowledged by the film.

In the days following my first viewing of *Midsommar*, I began to realise the power that horror held. Many people will tell you that mental health issues are akin to living in a horror every day—I can certainly say that at the height of my mental health problems, every day was the worst day of my life. Horror deals with the worst days of people's lives, and the darkest parts of people's psyches, so I began exploring how we might use it to reflect the difficulties of living with mental ill-health.

I am not the first person to have this realisation, nor was Ari Aster. Many modern filmmakers are creating what Adrian Lobb dubs 'allegorical horror' (2020) to represent struggles with trauma and mental ill-health. Remi Weekes' *His House* (2020) and Aster's debut feature *Hereditary* (2018) both employ hauntings in the home-setting to represent guilt and trauma; Jordan Peele's *Get Out* (2017) and Misha Green's *Lovecraft Country* (2020) both use horror elements to reflect the collective and individual traumas associated with racism; both *Carrie* (1976) and *The VVitch* (2015) use witchcraft to reflect toxic familial relationships and the effects of childhood abuse. All these screenplays are profoundly moving and deeply powerful. While none of them present us with easy answers about how the world could be improved, they all leave us with questions about how we see and interact with the people in our lives and the society that we inhabit.

What is it exactly, apart from horror, that all these films have in common? Why do they work so well? The answer leads us back into horror's history, particularly two key concepts from the Victorian Gothic tradition: metaphoric imagery, and the use of the uncanny.

You're coming out of a rehearsal. You are tired, but the sort of wired tired where you don't feel tired anymore. You feel like static electricity around an open grounding cable. You feel like a can of off-brand pop that's been shaken. You have not slept more than four hours in several months. You instead lie awake at night wondering how you ever managed to sleep before, convulsing in mental and physical pain as you half-remember things no one should have to remember, and imagine things worse than the things you half-remember.

As you cross the foyer towards the building's exit, you see a woman in a café drinking a coffee. She has a jack-o-lantern for a head. You double-back, and she does not. The light is orange, you tell yourself your imagination is overactive, and that you've been watching too many shitty '80s movies.

You leave and walk towards your car. There are two people in front of you, carrying heavy tools and chatting. You begin to worry that they will hurt you with their heavy tools; wonder what you would do if they turned around to attack. You slow down and stop, pretend to look at some scenery until they are far enough away. You do not have to worry for long though, because the matrix breaks, and they stop moving. They glitch in place. You can see their legs moving, still hear them laughing and chatting, but they are stuck as if they've met an invisible wall in an old PlayStation game. You step towards them, and they remain where they are. You move to get a look at them from a different angle, and they stay there, stuck in place, walking with no momentum.

Freud (1919) describes the uncanny as un-homely, or 'unfamiliar'—a sense that things are not quite as they should be. It appears that humans have evolved with a heightened awareness of the uncanny to assist in identifying and avoiding danger in their surroundings. Moosa & Ud-Dean (2010, pg.13) give the example of seeing a large number of dead insects on the floor—while in modern times that may mean that a swarm of bees came in through your open attic window and got trapped, the primal part of our subconscious looks for the toxic gas or poisoned water and, not seeing it, we begin to panic; we become afraid because we don't know what we should be afraid of. The uncanny was a hallmark of classic Gothic literature and is still widely used today. A prime example of this is Chris spotting Georgina the housekeeper staring seemingly vacantly out of the window towards the beginning of *Get Out*: before we truly understand who Georgina is and her place in the narrative, both Chris and the audience are placed in Uncanny Valley. We couldn't necessarily explain what isn't right about what we're seeing, but we understand that what we are seeing is both unsettling and potentially noxious. When I was pseudo-hallucinating pumpkin heads and glitches in the matrix, my mind was trying to manufacture its own uncanny valley. In my subconscious mind, nowhere was safe, and my conscious determination to pursue a normal life forced my brain's hand – if I wasn't going to acknowledge the danger for myself, it was going to make it so I couldn't avoid it anymore. The uncanny is about taking what is familiar and making it less so, a sense of displacement from what is real and what is safe, an experience common to many individuals living with mental ill-health.

How do we then capitalise on this sense of uncanny and displacement to show our audiences how our protagonist is feeling and engaging with the world around them? The answer lies in another commonly used facet of Gothic literature: metaphoric imagery. To put it simply, metaphoric imagery is an image or a set of images used to represent an emotion, feeling or idea. When we use metaphor, we engage the human mind in a different way. Will Storr (2019, pg45) explains how, when one scientific study asked participants to read the words 'he had a rough day', parts of their brains associated with feeling rough textures were activated. When asked to read 'he had a bad day,' the neural response was not as pronounced. If I say to you now, that having bad anxiety feels very worrying or unpleasant, you will have an understanding of worry and an understanding of unpleasant things—you won't necessarily have an understanding, unless you have lived with severe anxiety, of what is worrying or unpleasant about anxiety specifically. If I tell you that living with severe anxiety feels like having thousands of thumbtacks raining on your head and back, suddenly I place you in a physical situation that you can have an imagined response to. You begin to feel what is worrying and unpleasant.

You're probably familiar with the *Midsommar* Easter Egg that the face of Dani's dying sister can be seen in the trees during the May Queen celebrations (Squires, 2019). Dani's hallucinations and these hidden images are Aster's nod to both the metaphorical and the uncanny. I had no idea of this at the time of watching, though I understood that the face in the dark during her first trip was meant to be a dead family member. Much of our audience won't understand exactly what it is that we are trying to achieve—nor should they have to. I did not understand what my pseudo-hallucinations were trying to tell me, but I knew that I was afraid, and I understood that something in my life needed to change. Sometimes it is enough to present people with images and let the little bits of their minds that light up in brain scans tell them how they should respond to it. Sometimes it is better that we feel before we know. None of the films I've mentioned present us with concrete answers, but in this way they make us ask questions.

> *Your friends try to help. They try to encourage you, ask you how you're doing. They ask if you're sure it's just trauma—they tell you they know someone who has BPD and what you're going through sounds really similar to that. They tell you one of their friends has bipolar and doesn't it seem weird that you're just so up and down? They tell you that they know people with anxiety, and it doesn't really look like what's going on with you—doesn't trauma have loads of anxiety?*

> *You begin to drown in a myriad of labels and half-science. Good intentions become hours of tedium, justifying how you feel and how you are —versus how you should be—behaving. It's almost worse now that you've admitted there's a problem. Everyone keeps telling you that you have a chance to heal, that you can express yourself now, but your expressions come with a thousand explanations and a thousand new and unhelpful solutions.*

> *No one is willing to say that sometimes, you just hurt, and when you hurt you do things that no one understands, and that your growth will be about learning to navigate that hurt. It seems they get to the 'things that no one understands' and they're stuck there, like those two men walking in place.*

Midsommar is not without its faults. Mary Beth McAndrews (2019) highlights that its presentation of Dani's sister Terri's bipolar disorder is not as forgiving as Dani's unlabelled trauma—where Dani is emotional and sympathetic, Terri is the voiceless perpetrator of a murder-homicide, suggesting those with a bipolar diagnosis are 'homicidal burdens'. While I would argue neither come out well in the end – with Dani offering her ex-boyfriend up to be burned alive—I can understand that naming a disorder and then immediately demonising the person with said disorder is not appropriate. It's not even really necessary to name the condition that Terri lives with – many millions of people have lived with bipolar disorder and killed neither themselves nor their families, so her diagnosis is almost irrelevant to her behaviour. While it serves as an easy backstory, and an explanation for why Dani is so worried, there was almost certainly a way of presenting Terri's narrative without mentioning her diagnosis. (I am aware of the theory that Terri and Dani's parents were murdered, but since that has never been confirmed, I think McAndrews' point is valid and worth discussing.)

As I found myself, misunderstanding of mental ill-health is rife. There is no one way to experience mental ill-health, and even people with the same diagnoses can present very differently. It's no wonder then, in the age of search engines and online diagnostic criteria, that everyone considers themselves an expert. Self-stigmatisation is considered to be one of the biggest barriers to effective treatment and recovery from mental ill-health (Borenstein, 2020). How we hear people talk about the things we live with—as in the example of bipolar above—affects how we see ourselves. It affects how we feel we fit into society. It affects how we see our chances of success in life. So, when people get it wrong, and when people misrepresent us, we begin to feel alienated. When people think we're dangerous when we aren't, we begin to feel hopeless. Horror has got a lot wrong over the years and I don't have enough words left to go into that now, but I'm sure you can think of a few examples yourself; the opening of *Halloween* (2018) with patients wrapped in straight jackets, chained to posts, giggling, and barking like dogs, is an example that still leaves a nasty taste in my mouth.

Seeing representations of yourself is important. We need to fund people willing to write on behalf of themselves, and those willing to give a voice to those who can't or don't want to write. We need to create a robust culture of empathy and research around the work we make. A study from Blignault et al. (2010) found that, after attending a play designed to target mental health stigma in a Macedonian community in Australia, 59% of people who attended said that there would be a positive (or compassionate) reaction towards someone with a mental health issue in their community, compared to 11% before the experiment. It also found that people were more likely to access healthcare after seeing the play, this is potentally because the play represented the real-life experience of living within that particular community, which many audience members felt added to their experience of the play. The people in the audience felt acknowledged, and therefore compelled to act as a result.

This is true of people everywhere. People need to see people like them—people going through the same things that they're going through—to feel less alone and to challenge their self-stigma. Empowering people with visions of themselves helps them to show others what they need, and express how they feel when words just don't seem to be enough. It offers insights for people who haven't lived through the horrors. It gives people lucky enough to have never struggled with mental ill-health a way of seeing life from another perspective. At its best, it begins to spark conversations about ways of moving forward, ways of helping and ways of addressing the horrors of mental ill-health with compassion and empathy.

> *You try to tell people how you feel. You say you're in pain, you say you're hurting, you say that you can't help being like this right now. You say that you can't live like this anymore. They don't understand.*
>
> *Then you write. You write characters with your face, silently suffering through horrors unmanageable. You write and your words scream. They begin to understand.*
>
> *Then you write horrors for other people, with other people's faces. You talk to people, and you hear their voices, and their voices sit inside your words. The words scream, and people understand.*
>
> *Then you try to help other people scream. And you hope that they do. And you hope that the people that they write for understand.*

Horror is more than a genre. Horror is a tool.

References

Borenstein, J. (2020) 'Stigma, Prejudice and Discrimination Against People with Mental Illness', *American Psychiatric Association* [Online]. Available at: https://www.psychiatry. org/patients-families/stigma-and-discrimination (Accessed on 30th June 2021).

Blignault, I.; Smith, S.; Woodland, L.; Ponzio, V.; Ristevski, D. & Kirov, S. (2010) 'Fear and Shame: Using Theatre to Destigmatise Mental Illness in an Australian Macedonian Community' in *Health Promotion Journal of Australia*, 21(2), p.120-126.

Freud, S. (1919) 'The 'Uncanny" in Strachey, J. & Freud A. [Eds.] (1953) *The Standard Edition of the Complete Pyschological Works of Sigmund Freud*, Volume 17. London: The Hogarth Press & The Institute of Psychoanalysis.

GBD 2017 Disease and Injury Incidence and Prevalence Collaborators (2018). 'Global, regional, and national incidence, prevalence, and years lived with disability for 354 diseases and injuries for 195 countries and territories, 1990–2017: a systematic analysis for the Global Burden of Disease Study 2017', *The Lancet*, Vol.392, Iss.10159, pp.1789-1858.

Lane, C. (2019) 'How Midsommar Illustrates the Catharsis of Expressing Emotion', SyFy Wire [Online]. Available at: https://www.syfy.com/syfywire/how-midsommar-illustrates-the-catharsis-of-expressing-emotion (Accessed on June 29th 2021).

McAndrews, M. B. (2019) 'Midsommar takes a step forward and a step back in its portrayal of mental illness', Polygon [Online]. Available at: https://www.polygon. com/2019/7/16/20694958/midsommar-mental-illness-stereotypes-bi-polar-disorder-anxiety (Accessed on June 30th 2021).

Moosa, M. M. & Ud-Dean, M. (2010) 'Danger Avoidance: An Evolutionary Explanation of Uncanny Valley', *Biological Theory*, Vol.5, Iss.1, pp.12-14.

Ryan, D. (2019) "Midsommar': Ari Aster and Florence Pugh's Climactic Catharsis', / Film [Online]. Available at: https://www.slashfilm.com/midsommar-catharsis/ (Accessed on June 29th 2021).

Storr, W. (2019) The Science of Story-Telling. London: William Collins.

HORROR GAVE ME FREEDOM

ASHLEY D

What started as a fun way to spend the weekend turned into my love and passion. I remember the first time blood splatter went across the TV screen in *A Nightmare on Elm Street*. I couldn't sleep that night because I knew Freddy was going to find a way into my dreams. A killer that can haunt your dreams? How iconic. I think at the time, I really connected with Freddy. In the dreamlike world, he was untouchable, but in the real-life world, he was vulnerable. When you're young, you hold onto those dreams not knowing what life has in store for you. You are vulnerable, and I felt like Freddy has that sense to him in an odd way. I fell in love and I was hooked! *Halloween* (1978), *IT* (1990), *The Texas Chainsaw Massacre* (1974), and many more graced the TV screen. My pre-teens were already a weird time for me, but horror always had fun, laughter, and excitement in store.

One of my childhood best friends who lived down the road from me was the one I watched all my "firsts" with. I remember I would ride my go-kart to her house almost every single day after school so we could watch movies. Entering her house was one of my favorite things to do: her mother kept the house decorated for Halloween all year 'round - I always felt at home there. This is where it all began, the late-night horror movie binges and my love for anything and everything spooky. I could love Halloween all year, not just during October? I could actually "love" horror movies? This was all so new to me, but I knew it made me happy, and it was right for me. Little did I know that some years later I would hide that part away out of fear.

High school. A lot changed. Looking back, I am not quite sure of the timeline of events, but I remember feeling as though I could never be myself. There was the fear of judgment and ridicule from everyone. If you weren't wearing the latest fashion trends from Abercrombie or wore the same shirt twice that week, you were "nothing." If you weren't hanging with the popular kids, you were a loser. If you didn't have a significant other, you were seen as "unwanted." Don't even get me started on the pressures of sex, drinking, partying, and drugs. And if you liked horror movies or dressed in all black, you were one of the "goth" kids who worshiped Satan. It was such an eye-opening experience for me in the sense that no matter what I would do, what I would wear, or what I would act like, there was a "label" for me somewhere. It wasn't one I could choose myself either. Someone would look at me and say "you're 'this.'" I hated the thought of it, and due to that, I got scared. I didn't want to be labeled. I didn't want to be judged. So, I protected myself as best as I could: I didn't watch as many horror movies, and my friend group changed. It was really as simple as that. Despite this, I yearned for Halloween-inspired things every single day.

Living with this, I have graduated college, married the love of my life, officially moved into our first home, landed my first big girl job, and bought a dog. Life was going as it should, or how others (particularly in the South) feel it should be. That was when "the shift" happened for me. The time during your mid to late twenties when you question everything revolving around yourself: your choices, who you are, what you like, what you don't like, etc. I remember thinking that I hadn't felt "myself" in quite some time, and I didn't know why. I wanted to explore this, but I wasn't sure how.

I don't remember exactly what I was doing or thinking, but I decided I wanted to pick up body painting and special effects makeup. I had always loved working with makeup but found the desire to challenge myself in a whole different way. I saw some YouTube videos and a couple of my friends doing some really cool work, and I decided to go for it. For whatever reason, I kept thinking to myself, "This is me. This is everything I've always wanted." I yearned to learn how to transform myself into characters. I wanted to create beautiful, fun, and scary creatures with my own hands. I knew this was the key that would unlock where I had buried the "real" Ashley all those years before.

In order to get ideas on new characters and creatures for my makeup, I turned to the one thing I knew that would give me answers: horror movies. They had always provided something for me in the past, so why wouldn't they now? I fell in love again. Movie after movie after movie, I was hooked just like all those years before. From *The Exorcist* (1973) to *World War Z* (2013) to *The Nun* (2018), I was absorbing it all like a sponge. I was happy again. All the memories of hanging out with my childhood best friend, her Halloween-decorated house, and all the slasher classics came flooding back. It was like the movies kept reminding me of how much fun we had and how much I truly enjoyed being "scared." There was a beauty to it - a connection. The literal next day, I went to Goodwill and found all the vintage and Halloween décor I could find and slowly began decorating my house like the haunted Victorian house of my dreams. I got my very first tattoo on Friday the 13th (a pumpkin), I collected my first horror art piece, I played tons of horror video games, read horror books of all genres, and even got a subscription to a horror movie website. I was happy. For the first time since my pre-teens, I felt free. I felt like me. Horror gave me freedom.

I wanted to tell my story because, whether you like horror or not, you can relate in some way, shape, or form. At different points in our lives, we hide bits, and pieces of ourselves to fit in or surrender to the societal pressures we are all feeling from our parents, peers, or friend groups. We get scared of judgment and do whatever we can to feel safe and secure. Any human would do this; it's in our nature to protect ourselves. However, at some point the parts of us we hid away start screaming to be let out. We must listen. Let those bits of yourself free.

You will find the "freedom" you had been looking for all along. I am glad I listened. I am the freest I have ever been. I am more myself than ever before and it's all because of horror. Horror doesn't let up, it doesn't hold back, and it doesn't care, something I needed to desperately learn how to do for myself at the time. Horror also exists on its own terms. It doesn't have limitations holding it back from anything: it just "is." You can accept it for what it is or not accept it. Either way, it keeps going — another aspect I needed to learn for myself. At that time, I needed to learn how to just live and not care about what people thought of me. Lastly, horror taught me about fighting back. When I think about life, at the end of it all, I want to be labeled as the "Final Girl." The girl that never gave up and kept fighting despite the many ways life, the killer, had tried to bring her down. That despite all the fear and challenges, I kept going. Throw them out the window. This is the most loving community I have ever been a part of. We all were those kids who hid pieces of ourselves away out of fear. We all were terrified of judgment from our peers. We were the weird kids. However, we took that fear and turned it into love and acceptance. We all eventually find that one thing in life that sets us free, ours just happens to be horror.

I want to give a huge shout-out to the horror community for all they have done for me. They took me in with open arms and fully accepted me for who I was without question. They have been an incredible source of good energy, love, and passion. Whatever "things" you've heard about those of us who love horror, throw them out the window. This is the most loving community I have ever been a part of. We all were those kids who hid pieces of ourselves away out of fear. We all were terrified of judgment from our peers. We were the weird kids. However, we took that fear and turned it into love and acceptance. We all eventually find that one thing in life that sets us free, ours just happens to be horror.

TO BE BLACK AND LOVE HORROR

DESTINY KELLY

Content Warning: Racism.

Finishing school and entering the adult world is always an unnerving time in one's life, especially for people like me, a Black visual artist, who is pursuing a career in the arts. Being in my early twenties with dreams of having a professional career in the horror industry, it is quite intimidating, but what keeps me motivated is my desire to be a part of the growing Black representation in the horror genre. For the majority of my life, I have yearned for inclusion in the horror spaces that I love so much, and there has always been a great need for more diversity in horror, especially for Black women. It wasn't until I became an adult that I met other Black women horror creators, many of whom are actually getting amazing opportunities to share their art with the world. It is great to start seeing more representation now, but I always wish I had more of that as a child. However, I am eternally grateful for the small amount of Black representation in horror films I did see growing up because it made me feel less alone and opened my eyes to the positive impact that horror media can have on the Black community.

When I was a young child, my sister and I spent a lot of our time at home watching movies. At that age, I didn't really understand the concept of representation. What I did know was that the women in so many of the films I watched were always just supporting characters, or worse, sexualized objects who served no real purpose to the plot. All of those poor depictions of women in film became the norm for me, and I never expected much of anything else. That is until I watched my very first horror film. I was only about five years old when my sister and I raided our dad's VHS collection, and there it was: a blood red cover, a burned horror villain rocking a fedora, and a badass teenage girl. Wes Craven's classic slasher film, *A Nightmare on Elm Street* (1984), was my first dose of horror greatness, and despite being way too young to watch it, I was obsessed. I loved that Freddy Krueger was such a fun and entertaining killer, but the real reason this film drew me in and kept me coming back for more was its final girl, Nancy Thompson.

Nancy was the first woman film character I ever saw, who was completely in control of her own narrative, faced her fears, and courageously fought the villain. In my little eyes, the horror genre became the place where it was possible for women to be leaders, to be strong, and to be fearless. It was a small slice of the representation that I had been unknowingly craving, and as I began my journey into the world of horror, I discovered more and more women who got to be the heroes in their stories. However, there was still one huge problem. While I could relate to these films through my gender identity, the absence of Black women in those roles was disturbingly clear. None of the leading women in the horror films I watched looked like me, and at such a young age I just mindlessly accepted that Black women didn't get to be in such roles.

A few years later, around 8 years old, a lot of my extended family began to take notice of my love for horror. My uncle, who is a horror enthusiast himself, was so joyful when he found out that I was into these films. He would always exclaim that he'd never seen a child as young as me who was fascinated by scary things, and he wanted to help me expand my horror knowledge outside some of the more mainstream films and franchises I'd already seen. Every so often he would lend me a couple of horror films from his DVD collection, and one week he happened to include the film that would finally make me feel seen and forever shape the way I viewed horror.

Among this stack of borrowed DVDs was *The Craft* (1996), and I remember being so excited to slide that disc into my DVD player at home. A film centered around a group of teen girl witches felt like it was made just for me, and to my pleasant surprise, one of those witches was a Black girl. The cherry on top was that she wasn't a minor character whose existence in the film revolved around negative tropes or racial stereotypes, like so many other Black characters in horror. A stereotypical character is not a real representation, and I was never able to truly identify with any horror characters through my Blackness until I saw Rachel True as Rochelle in *The Craft*.

I was thrilled to see that Rochelle was not just a member of the friend group, but blew my mind even more, however, was that Rochelle's challenge was the racism she faced from her peers at school. This struck me so hard, because what

Rochelle was experiencing in the film heavily mirrored my own experiences. For most of my academic life, I was often the only Black girl in so many spaces. I'd been facing racism and microaggressions from both teachers and peers as early as Kindergarten. It's absolutely heartbreaking that any five-year-old has to experience something so awful in a space where they should be able to feel safe and have fun learning. This feeling only grew worse the older I got, because it was easier to understand and identify the racist microaggressions when they happened. It is always scary being the only Black person in the room, because I inevitably have to enter that space knowing that there will be people who refuse to welcome me in.

In *The Craft*, Rochelle is constantly taunted by a group of girls in her swim class. Rochelle's racist bully, Laura, is fully aware of her privilege and knows that even their swim coach will do nothing more than carelessly tell her to "knock it off." There are no consequences for her actions, because as a white person, she holds power in the spaces she occupies. Rochelle is just trying to be herself and succeed within this space by nailing her dives, but Laura continuously makes her feel like she doesn't belong. When I watched this film for the first time, I was in the third grade, which was around the time I started shifting into "GATE" (Gifted and Talented Education) classes for students who excelled in their studies. This also meant that I was transitioning to learning environments where I would often be the only Black person in the room. I quickly realized that these spaces were not very welcoming of people who looked like me. So many people doubted me and wanted to see me fail, watching Rochelle be treated this way by her classmates really hit close to home during that time in my life.

Another important aspect of the film is how Rochelle's friends are aware of her experience, but are oblivious to how it affects her self-esteem and her ability to see the beauty in her Blackness. I have also been the only Black person in a lot of my friend groups throughout life, and it is true that so many of my friends were not the best allies. It is never enough to just not be racist. A lack of knowledge about Black culture and history, along with remaining silent and turning a blind eye to the racism of others, is just as harmful. In one scene, Rochelle's friend Sarah is demonstrating to the group her ability to transform parts of her body including changing her hair color. Rochelle, in a moment of awe, excitedly begs Sarah to turn her hair blonde. Even though Rochelle has already gotten revenge against Laura at this point in the film, she is obviously still suffering from the racism she endured. Like Rochelle, not only did I lack acceptance into the communities I was a part of, but I lacked the proper allyship I needed in a lot of my inner circles.

Nothing can fully heal my racial trauma, but the scene in the film where Rochelle's spell against Laura finally takes effect is always such a cathartic moment for me. At 8 years old, seeing Rochelle make that flawless dive into the water while Laura suffered her fate made me feel like I too had the power to overcome anyone who tried to hold me back, and that I could continue to shine even when I had no one to look to for support. *The Craft* helped me realize just how substantial the horror genre could be in examining the real-life horrors that Black people face every single day. Horror has always been an outlet that artists of all backgrounds use to connect with others, address our fears, and explore ways to move forward when life presents us with terrifying obstacles. The immense catharsis that the genre invokes in audiences can be so healing, and Black people deserve the same level of release for all of the pain we have endured throughout history. We deserve Black Horror that gives us a sense of empowerment in a world that so often tries to break us down.

As my childhood flew by, my hopes for more representation in the genre continued, and I started to develop an even deeper love for horror in my teenage years. I finally decided in high school that I wanted to be a horror creator and eventually pursue a career in horror filmmaking. I became incredibly passionate about it, but there was still something holding me back and filling me with doubt. Even though there were more Black women characters on screen each year that I could relate to, I didn't yet know of any Black women who were actually making horror media and content. The lack of representation behind-the-scenes in horror made me feel like there was still no place for me within it.

Eventually, I did discover a few Black women creating incredible things in the genre, but that still was not enough to boost my self-esteem. It wasn't until I was a young adult, thanks to social media platforms like Twitter, that I finally found my people. I met so many wonderful, talented Black women who are horror fans, content creators, and filmmakers. Coincidentally, during that same time there was a huge boom in the conversation of Black Horror after the success of Jordan Peele's 2017 film *Get Out*. The horror community had become one of the most influential communities in my life, and the increasing Black representation in the genre was so important to me. It is important to me because there is still so much work to be done. We need to make sure that future generations of horror obsessed Black children grow up feeling included in all areas of the genre. Childhood is such a pivotal time in which seeing oneself accurately represented in the media can be most influential. I can't help but think how much easier finding my place in the horror community would have been if I grew up with the same amount of representation that white children get. To have proper representation, Black people have to get the chance to tell our own stories, and people need to support us when we do. We are doing the work, writing the screenplays, and making the pitches. We are flowing with endless original and creative ideas that the world has yet to see. It is up to people with privilege in the horror community to not speak for us, but to amplify our voices and help open doors to the opportunities that Black people are working so hard to get. Every opportunity given to a Black person is a chance for them to inspire and be a familiar face for future generations of Black horror fans.

Black horror filmmakers, including beginners like myself, strive to tell the stories that we have always wanted to see, the kinds of stories that we didn't get to see ourselves in while growing up. We want to see ourselves as the vigorous villains, the creatures of the night, and the heroic final girls who are driving the plot forward. Black women and non-binary horror creators especially need our voices to be heard. Companies, outlets, and platforms too often settle for giving all opportunities to Black men in the name of diversity, but refuse to seek any further representation. As a Black woman, I no longer want to be overlooked, and I no longer want to be an afterthought. We cannot have true diversity in horror until we are seeing ourselves just as much as we see the white men who have dominated the genre for far too long.

There are Black women of all levels of expertise creating horror films that provide fresh perspectives on a variety of subjects. From small indie filmmakers like myself who are writing and directing horror shorts based on our own personal experiences, to established filmmakers like Nia DaCosta who brought a beloved horror slasher back to life in *Candyman* (2021), a big studio film with timely themes that resonate with the Black community as a whole. These new perspectives have the power to spark important conversations and can undoubtedly leave a huge impact on all horror fans. Black women are here, we have always been here, and it is time for us to be seen, supported, and celebrated for our significant contributions to the genre.

BONE BEGETS BLOOD: A PERSONAL HISTORY OF HORROR FROM THE LAB TO THE CINEMA

KC AMIRA

Content Warnings: child death, visceral gore

The vulture spread its wings wide, kicking up sand in violent puffs. Each muscle in its back spasmed as it lifted itself off the ground and perched in a nearby tree amongst its kin, carrying with it a bit of pig entrails in its beak. I rarely caught the birds in action, pecking away at the bloated bellies of the sows we were using to research human decomposition along the Migrant Trail in the Sonoran Desert, kissed on each side by Mexico and Arizona. The work of the birds was known only through the tell-tale signs of scavenging they left behind in the night—a missing eye, a humerus bone drying feet away in the sun. Pouring through the hidden camera footage from the night before was like watching a film you didn't know was going to be a horror until the coyotes came out to play.

Before venturing into a PhD focused on horror cinema, I worked in a world that dealt in a different kind of horror—I worked directly with the remains of the dead. It started as a deep fascination with the afterlife, one developed from watching horror films over the back of the sofa while my mother assumed I was asleep in my room. I was less concerned about the idea of the soul and whether it existed; my fear of the visceral and the tangible overpowered my fear of the wandering ghost. I wanted to know what happened to our bodies when we died, what took place after Jason plunged his knife into a co-ed's chest and she collapsed into the brush of the wood. The interest could have taken me down a multitude of different paths—mortuary work or work in the medical field, both of which I considered. Instead, I chose a path once less travelled but now popularised by television shows like *Bones* and *CSI Miami*. I wanted to learn everything I could about body decomposition, to see what happened to Jason's victims on the silver screen in real life. Call it morbid curiosity, fascination, or a red flag, but nothing called me as strongly as working with the dead, particularly those whose voices needed amplification post-mortem: the lost, the violated and the murdered.

My first venture into working with the dead began within the pages of books. I explored endless funerary traditions like endocannibalism, the consumption of the deceased, and dove more deeply into the practices of my own Mayan ancestors. My unique interest landed me several spots at conferences and lecture series, as who does not want to know more about a tribe that comes together to eat the flesh of their loved one? Yet drowning in words just wasn't enough—I needed to make contact somehow, to absorb the energy of the dead themselves and find some way in which to communicate with them the way I'd seen in horror films; not through seances or fortune tellers, but through that moment of physical contact that translates into a story to be told. This desire led me to Transylvania, where I spent four weeks in an osteoarchaeological program analysing the remains of the long-dead, allowing the etchings left on their bones to speak to me about the lives they had lived. These etchings told tales of poverty, disease, status and, once for a fleeting moment, suspected foul play. This was the story I had been looking for. I needed to know more about that moment when life was lost, when the final words were spoken, the final breath taken. In a horror film, we know the knife-wielder, the strangler, and the menace, whether they are revealed at the beginning or the end. This was a different kind of horror story, one where the perpetrator was not hiding just out of sight, one where the traces left behind were nearly invisible. Ancient remains could weave a beautiful narrative, but the remains of the untimely departed needed an urgent attention I couldn't ignore. I packed my bags for London, off to dive even deeper into the work of the dead through a degree in Forensic Anthropology at the University College London, and the relationship between my love of cinematic gore and my passion for understanding the post-mortem body began to change.

Horror films, particularly those of the slasher and body horror variety, have a history of being deemed 'exploitative'. The *Saw* franchise has been overanalysed and deconstructed, its morals and role in cinema as torture porn called into question by academics and the horror blogger alike. Working directly with the dead, with gore much more delicate than anything I had seen in *A Nightmare on Elm Street*, gave me a new approach to the way I viewed death onscreen. The dead command of you a certain respect when working with the people connected to them, who grieve for them, who want answers. The idea of death I once held closely transitioned from mere fascination to duty, and I felt a new disdain for shock value, for blood for blood's sake. I knew images such as these elicited trauma responses from survivors of the dead. Was my love for body horror exploitative in itself? Was I dancing on some moral tightrope where I had to choose one fascination over the other? I toyed with this conundrum for two years, through two masters' dissertations in which I studied the remains of children who had died from disease, poverty or had become victims of child abuse. I could no longer watch *Sleepaway Camp* without thinking of the remains of dead children boxed away at the Office of the Chief Medical Examiner in New York City where I watched my first autopsy (it was a double – go big or go home). I deeply contemplated this binary view of death, and whether I could aid the dead and still indulge in the big screen violent visceral transgressions I had enjoyed in my youth. It wasn't a study of Immanuel Kant, John Rawls or Diogenes that simplified this moral conflict; it was a late-night eBay tour that ended in the purchase of a classic, highly underrated VHS documentary.

American makeup artist Tom Savini is a household name for the horror savvy, known for his ground-breaking use of special effects to bring us the blood and gore the '70s and '80s horror fanatics have come to adore. From Kevin Bacon's arrow in the throat in *Friday the 13th* to Ted Danson's aquatic-zombie corpse in *Creepshow*, these iconic moments have shaped the way that we look at death and visceral transformation on screen. What only some know of Savini is where he got the inspiration to create such realistic and brutal imagery—his time as a photographer in the Vietnam War. Damon Santostefano's 1982 documentary *Tom Savini: Master of Horror Effects* on *Volume 1 of Scream Greats* details Savini's career, starting from his trauma-riddled time in the jungles of Vietnam, which he coyly refers to as a "...real lesson in anatomy." Savini used the horrors he saw in the field to inspire the work that has labelled him a guru of the special effects craft. If he could somehow bridge the gap between the two, why couldn't I?

I had always been a fan of Savini—in my early college years, I considered taking a hiatus and attending his special effects make-up program in Monessen, Pennsylvania, just outside of Pittsburgh. Were it not for money, I would have seen myself in a different kind of laboratory, creating my own brand of gore without questioning whether having seen the real thing would have somehow made me a better artist, or given me a better understanding of the way we depict death on screen. I've never seen the type of gore Savini saw or experienced the extreme shell shock of the horrors of war. I never saw anything more gruesome than decomposing pigs, crime scene photos and a handful of autopsies, some of which were conducted on bodies that had long begun to fuse with the soil. Yet a relationship with the dead is one nonetheless, and it was that physical connection to human remains and the residual sadness I felt when packing the bones of long-dead children back into boxes that led me to look at death from a new perspective. I removed myself from the lab and set up shop in front of both the television and the movie screen. Like Savini, I wanted to attempt to meld reality with fiction. Would understanding the weight of a three-year old's scapula in my hand shine a different light on Gage's death in Stephen King's *Pet Sematary*? Would the post-mortem tomography scans of deceased children I was meant to pour over for research's sake make me place a higher value on the life of Ed's son Billy in *Pumpkinhead*?

"What saved me from going insane in Vietnam was looking at these horrible scenes like they were a special effect someone else had created," Savini said of his time as a war photographer. "I tried to disconnect from the horror and wondered how I could recreate it as a special effect myself." Could I do the same? I could, and I would seek and find safety from real-life horror within the horror of the cinema.

My deep, unfortunate knowledge of the anatomy of the death of a child, whether ancient or within the context of a modern-day case, flicked on the lights in rooms I never thought to access. I realised that the application of these dark truths to the way child death and violence are portrayed in horror films could shed some light on the way audiences receive images of child violence and violence against children, and what this means about the way we look at children in the real world. Bridging the gap could illuminate the potentials for the desensitization horror fans are accused of experiencing through indulgence in the genre and expose new sub-types of morbid curiosity that remained under-discussed. Yet more important than the knowledge that the fusion of my two passions could reveal was the preservation of my own mental health. In the cinema, I am not followed by the smell of decaying flesh, my hands are not covered in bone dust, nor do the medical records of syphilitic infants cover my desk. I can leave these dissections of child death and violence, blood, and gore, within the confines of a streaming service or a VHS cover weathered by the greasy fingers of the morbidly curious. One can grow numb watching the same Jason kills over and over, but you can never become immune to looking over the remains of a child whose life was taken too soon.

Every now and then, the smell of the desert overcomes me, and I feel the heat of the Sonoran sun, whether I am standing in line at a coffee shop or waiting for the shower water to get warm—these memories of death and loss have never left. I think often of the child's backpacks left alone behind the taupe boulders along the Migrant trail, shreds of Micky Mouse fabric hanging from the prickles of a jumping cactus. The pigs that we used during our study needed to be dressed in clothing to better understand the way a body left in the desert has vanished into the atmosphere, so we gave them the clothes of children. I could never separate the two, as I felt that watching the pig be taken by the desert was the same as watching it happen to a child. I carry the images of child-sized socks and shoes dusting the shrubs with me to this day. It is such horrors, both real and imagined, that pique our interest and allow us to unlock the darkest parts of ourselves. It is when linking the real and the imagined that we fully realise that our fears extend far beyond the blood and gore of the horror film, for they are rooted firmly in certainty. Throughout my time straddling these two different worlds, both deeply inundated with death, I discovered my own truth—I could not value reality over the imagined when it came to the work of the dead, for one begets the other, and that truth is inescapable.

BEING FRIENDS WITH THE DARK

MARINA GARRIDO

Content Warning: Child Abuse

Horror and I have been friends for a long time. As a child my favorite books were the ones about witches, werewolves, vampires, and monsters, which meant that the *Goosebumps* series occupied a large part of my shelves (it still does to this day). However, my relationship with horror began before I learned how to read or even how to tie my own shoes. My parents separated during my mother's pregnancy, and by the time I was born they were already divorced, and my mom had her own apartment. It was very amicable at first, my parents are both lawyers, so they handled the divorce paperwork together and agreed that I would live with my mom and my dad could see me on the weekends. When I was four years old, I overheard my dad telling his girlfriend how much he hated my stepfather and how his life would be so much better if he just killed my mom so that he could take full custody of me. I didn't tell anyone about what I heard, afraid that if I did my father would find out and immediately murder my mom. Soon it became obvious that there was something wrong with me: I begged my mom to not see my father on the weekend, and at school I would spend all of recess hiding inside the classroom, I thought my dad would come to kidnap me. He was around the school constantly because it was owned by my grandmother (his mom). At home I wouldn't let my mother out of my sight, not even to go to the bathroom, however, what convinced her to put me in therapy was when I told her that I wanted to die the same second that she did and be buried in the same coffin.

After two months I finally confessed to my therapist why I had become such a jumpy and morbid kid; of course she told my mom and both women reassured me that my father would never do something like that, but that I wasn't obligated to see him if I didn't want to. That did not sit well with him, and that was when the second phase of my nightmare began: my dad would show up at our apartment building and try to break in to get me. He would call my grandma's house (my mom's mom) and tell her to get ready for her daughter's funeral. This went on for a year until my father finally stopped (to this day I'm not sure why he stopped), thankfully he never managed to physically harm anyone, but he was successful in traumatizing me. I cut off contact with him completely, got pulled out of school for my own safety, went to therapy weekly until the age of nine and had constant nightmares. It came as a shock to my family that, as soon as I started to read, my favorite books were the "scary ones," but to me that made perfect sense: I wanted to read about people who had had experiences like mine.

Books like *Goosebumps* gave me the opportunity to read about kids that were just like me: they saw themselves in terrifying situations where they had to fight the monsters to keep themselves and their families safe. I found strength through those characters and those stories—they reassured me that I too could fight my monsters and win, but also that being scared of the monsters didn't mean that I was weak. I loved the fear that they made me feel because it was so different from the one that I was living with, the fear that horror gave me was electric and it was mixed with the thrill of knowing that even though it scared me I was reading it anyway. As a kid I was already so terrified of dying and getting hurt that I never learned how to swim, ride a bike, or climb a tree. None of those things mattered while I was buried under the covers with *Scary Stories to Tell in the Dark* or watching *When a Stranger Calls* (2006)—behind my mom's back of course, I was eight and really regretted that decision at bedtime—the only thing I felt was brave and powerful.

Power and freedom, those two fundamental things that everyone wants in one way or another, they make us feel safe and allow us to pursue a life that can make us happy. They are also the things that kids aren't allowed to have until, at least, the age of twelve; however, children tend to feel safe most of the time due to faith in their parent's ability to protect them. When that faith is shattered and you believe that your own father is the one that's going to murder the only parent you have keeping you safe, you are truly made aware of how powerless and vulnerable you are. Growing up, I knew exactly how powerless I was, and I knew that I couldn't do anything to protect myself or my mom if my dad ever decided he wanted to kill her, or me, again. The most wonderful gift that horror gave, and continues to give, me is the ability to restore my sense of power for a few hours at a time.

The two figures that showed me how powerful I could be one day when I got older were those of the Witch and the Final Girl. Personally, I always tended to lean more towards wanting to be the witch because their strength and power wasn't as passive as the final girl's who, even though incredibly strong and cunning, only reacted to what was done to her by the killer. The witch, on the other hand, could be the one to attack if someone wronged her, invaded her personal space, or threatened her in any way. As a kid, being able to exact revenge on the ones who hurt you and being capable of wielding so much power that people feared messing with you sounded like a dream come true. I wanted that power so badly that I longed to be a witch long before I ever saw *Harry Potter* (2001). I also tended to root for the witch in a lot of movies, especially if the main characters were making particularly dumb choices, and that concerned the adults around me to no end.

Skipping forward a little to the beginning of my teenage years we have a very angry 13-year-old Marina. I was pretty much the stereotype of the "emo scene kid" from the 2010's: screamed along to Simple Plan's lyrics, only wore black clothes paired with skull themed jewelry and so heavily bullied at school that I had to transfer. That was the age when I finally discovered my Holy Grail of Horror: Stephen King's books. I picked up his *Night Shift* collection at random one day at the bookstore (at the time King wasn't that widely known in Brasil) and, sure enough, that book was my gateway to the world of "adult" horror fiction. I devoured as many King novels as I could find, went to see as many horror movies as I could and scoured bookshop shelves for new books. Once again, when I found myself going through a rough time and needing something to hold onto, it was horror that helped me deal with it and kept me sane during the emotional roller-coaster from hell that is being a teenager.

Moving away to a different state for college at the age of eighteen seemed to me almost as scary as any of the *Insidious* (2010) movies (yes, I did find them terrifying, please don't judge me). Above all else, I feared not being able to make new friends and spending all those four years being the reject at the corner of the classroom. Not only did I manage to befriend incredible people during my very first week of classes, but they were also horror lovers, which meant that we constantly shared our spooky interests and went to see the latest horror movies after class. The thing that my mother had hoped to be just a phase was one of the reasons that I enjoyed college as much as I did. As literature majors, we were given a significant amount of freedom that allowed us to take any class we wanted, so of course every time I saw a subject that was even remotely connected to horror, I signed up for it. Sadly, my university was very elitist, so many of my teachers looked down on anything that wasn't considered "high literature" and scolded anyone that showed an appreciation for "commercial fiction".

Due to those circumstances, I had to settle for only a "origins of gothic fiction" class, however, I was lucky enough to have a young woman who had just gotten her master's degree come teach a horror movie class. Her subject was by far my favorite, she introduced me to so many incredible movies that I'd never have watched otherwise and provided us with several books/articles that discussed the construction of horror. There was just a small number of students in her class, around twenty people, so she would take us all to the movies and afterwards we would discuss how it related to what we'd studied so far. It was thanks to this wonderful woman and her refusal to let academia dictate what is and isn't worth teaching that I dared to write my thesis about King's short stories. For two years I lived and breathed Stephen King (both novels and non-fiction) and the more I studied the more I saw that writing about my life-long love of horror is what I wanted to do with my life.

Finally, an interesting thing happened while writing this essay: I realized that I consider horror books/movies to be more than just entertainment, they are also survival guides. As a very anxious person my brain insists on coming up with dangerous scenarios of all varieties: what if I get mugged at gunpoint? What if I move to an apartment that's haunted by a poltergeist? So, every time I read about demonic possession, or a zombie apocalypse, or even crazed serial killers I take notice of how the characters fight those threats and try to memorize their best strategies. Is that completely paranoid and insane? Yes, but hey, if we were dropped into a horror movie, I know I would last to the end. Ok, I wouldn't survive in a franchise like *A Nightmare on Elm Street* (1984) or *Friday the 13th* (1980), since I'm not able to run for more than a minute before passing out, but you can put me in any James Wan movie, and I guarantee that I would make it.

Ps: Please, don't put me in any kind of horror movie ever, I would cry and sacrifice myself for the dog.

HORROR IN THE CLOSET

LUCY DERRY-HOLMES

Content Warning: homophobia, sexual assault, death

Forever the underdog of cinema, horror and homosexuality has gone hand in hand dating as far back as our cult classic B movie icons, from James Whale's infamous telling of *Bride of Frankenstein* (1935), to the romantic era of the lesbian vampire *Dracula's Daughter* (1974), to now a modern horror renaissance of rejecting gender norms and the incorporation of intersectional feminism in the trailblazing *Assassination Nation* (2019). What do all these staples of horror have in common? The theme of villains, "otherness" and its attachment to queer theory.

Unlike any other genre, horror invokes so many queer readings and an avid love from the LGBTQ+ community because of its metaphorical (and at times physical) rejection of the heterosexual status quo. Henry Benshoof best describes this as:

> for the better part of the 20th century, queer people like vampires have rarely cast a reflection in the social looking glass of popular culture. When they are seen, they are often filtered through the iconography of a horror film. Both movie monsters and queer people have existed chiefly in shadowed closets and when they do emerge, they cause panic and fear. (Benshoff, 1974)

Robin Wood defines the theme of otherness as not only 'something external to the culture or to the self, but also as what is repressed (though never destroyed) in the self and projected outward in order to be hated and disowned'. He highlights that horror as a genre is the emergence of these repressed feelings and our struggle to keep them hidden from normality.

The history of LGBTQ+ film is bound up with social and political constraints, most significantly the Motion Picture Production Code often called the Hays Code of the 1930s. From 1934 to 1954 these guidelines prohibited or restricted the depiction of subject matters such as profanity, drugs, sexuality, and religious insolence; a motion picture was not to "lower the moral standards of those who see it" (Leff & Simmons, 2001). The strict Hays Code forbade explicit depictions of homosexuality on film for three decades (unless depicted to be punished or caricatured) during which there was a slew of queer-coded villains. Confronting erasure or demonization on-screen, queer viewers responded by reading between the lines for points of self-identification. Many of us can relate to the monster or the villain because at some point in our lives as queer people we have also been subjected to similar emotional and physical abuse because of something we cannot control. As the monster cannot control their outward appearance, we cannot control our sexuality.

Robin Wood continues this notion that homosexuality and bisexuality are evident in F.W Murnau's *Nosferatu* (1922) and James Whale's rendition of *Frankenstein* (1931), both of which include implied homosexuality as representative of heteronormative anxieties, meaning the "us" (the townspeople) and the "them" (the monsters). In 1942, during the height of monster horror films, *Cat People* was born. This Hays code era horror classic is one of the earliest examples of established "otherness", Directed by Jacques Tourneur, *Cat People* tells the story of Irena Dubrovna, who believes she is descended from a race of people who shapeshift into panthers when sexually aroused or angered. This is a physical manifestation of her fear that her repressed identity (being a lesbian) will be found out, a fear many of us within the LGBTQ+ community have experienced and continue to have to this day.

Richard Dyer argues that gothic literature and film, particularly of vampires, reflected society's attitudes towards gay and lesbian identities at the time. The vampire's private double life, the concealing of a secret, the stereotypical femininity of male vampires and the inherent eroticism and fetishisation of lesbians is very apparent. From the classics of the vampire genre such as *Daughters of Darkness* (1971), *The Vampire Lovers* (1970) and *Interview With A Vampire* (1994) to name but a few are very reflective of queer representation at the time.

When we speak about queer theory and the notion of queer coding in horror the infamous film portfolio of Alfred Hitchcock often comes to mind and the queer trope of "dandyism." Richard Allen describes the dandy as a complex figure who is "inherently homosexual, though not explicitly, can also be defined by the way that he combines feminine and masculine traits per the theories of gender that circulated in Hitchcock's youth where homosexuality was conceived in terms of male femininity" (Allen, 2007).

One of the clearest examples of queer coding in horror cinema is often referred to as *Rope* (1948) and the relationship between Brandon and Philip. The screenplay writer of *Rope* who also came out later in life Arthur Laurent confirms this, stating "what was curious to me was that *Rope* was obviously about homosexuals. The word was never mentioned. Not by Hitch, not by anyone at Warner's. It was referred to as 'it.' They were going to do a picture about 'it,' and the actors were 'it'". However, this was certainly not the first or last example of queer coded and often villainized characters in Hitchcock's repertoire. The widely recognised Norman Bates from *Psycho* (1960), Mrs. Danvers in *Rebecca* (1940) and Bruno in *Strangers On A Train* (1951) were all subject to queer coding, the trope of the queer killer and othered at the hands of Hitchcock and Hollywood. Caden Gardner (2018) states, "What is often the case with the queering of Hitchcock characters is that there is often something withheld, intangible, unknowable about their inner-lives." These characters of horror at the time are often portrayed as secretive, aloof, and oftentimes manipulative— instilling the fear of the homosexual agenda onto the audience and as a result get their comeuppance in the end, usually in the form of death, often referred to as the bury your gays trope.

Perhaps the most well-known and infamous trope of horror is that of sex kills, quite literally. A throwback to the strict guidelines of the Hays Code and the notion of no sex before marriage, this stereotype of the quintessential modern femme fatale can be seen time and time again in 80s slashers and still in horror cinema today. The promiscuous young woman who oozes sexuality gets what's coming to her in the form of gruesome death and often is usually the first victim at the hands of the killer. So how does this relate to queer theory? The trope of sex kills and homosexuality is most evidently seen in *A Nightmare on Elm Street Part 2: Freddy's Revenge* (1985), argued to be one of the gayest horror films ever made. Our protagonist Jesse can be seen to become increasingly unhinged and violent as his homoerotically-coded connection to Kreuger strengthens, suggesting his sexuality isto be ashamed of and repressed and as a result to be forever tormented by an equally queer coded character, Freddy Kreuger.

It's important to recognise, unlike any other genre, horror showcases the raw complexities of everyday life and the true horror of what it means to be human. You will struggle to find any other style of film that deals with the very real themes of misogyny, homophobia, mental health, sexual assault, and grief (albeit not always in a positive light) as openly and honestly. A more recent film that immediately springs to mind for me and one I hold very dear to my heart is the often overlooked but now a cult classic amongst the LGBTQ+ community *Jennifer's Body* (2009). Director Karyn Kusama has been very outspoken in recent years of this film being the perfect example of Hollywood marketing gone wrong. Promoted as a "horny horror flick for teenage boys" starring Megan Fox, who at the time was at the height of her career and unapologetically harassed and sexualised by mainstream media during the era of *Transformers*, this film was quite ahead of its time. A canonically bisexual character, Jennifer turns the trope of the overtly sexual teen who we assume at the start of the film will be assaulted at the hands of the band Low Shoulder instead turns the trope on its head as she becomes a succubus and uses her sexuality to lure men as her prey to maintain her beauty and youth. Throughout the film, there is very clear sexual tension between Jennifer and Needy, and as a young queer female still figuring herself out at the time I felt so seen by this film. The "will they won't they?" and falling in love with your best friend experience is one many of us can relate to. Both Jennifer and Needy represent two very different sides to queerness and sexuality. Needy is still shy, unsure of herself and her relationship with both Jennifer and her boyfriend Chip. Whilst Jennifer is so unapologetically herself, knows she is objectified and uses this to her advantage, she has no shame in admitting her feelings towards Needy. Megan Fox goes on to describe her experience playing Jennifer as, "I think what I loved about the movie is it's so unapologetic and how completely inappropriate it is at all times. That was my favourite part about the script and the character. It's fun to be able to say the shit that she got to say and get away with it and how people find it charming."

In recent years this has been taken a step further with films such as *The Perfection* (2018), *Velvet Buzzsaw* (2018) and *What Keeps You Alive* (2018), all of which tell tales of LGBTQ+ characters where their sexuality is not at the forefront of the plot. It is part of who they are but is not their sole personality trait, a much-needed breath of fresh air. In addition, this can be seen in *Assassination*

109

Nation (2019) and *Bit* (2019) in the representation of trans characters, specifically trans women where the subject of their gender is not questioned or ridiculed, and most importantly the characters being portrayed by trans actors, specifically trans women where the subject of their gender is not questioned or ridiculed, and most importantly the characters being portrayed by trans actors themselves.

As we enter the new era of the roaring 20' and a world post-global pandemic, what can we hope to see for horror in the years to come? I feel we are in a horror revival, even in the past five years horror has come leaps and bounds with modern directors paving the way such as Ari Aster, Jordan Peele, and Nia DaCosta in the ways of storytelling, pushing the envelope with complex characters, bigger budgets, and more artistic freedom. We have come leaps and bounds in the representation of queer people, our fears and our relationships when comparing to the era of the Hays Code; however, we still have a long way to go.

Space needs to be given for stories of queer people to be told by queer people, particularly those of intersectional identities often overlooked in western society such as Black trans women and non-binary individuals. Too long have our stories been told from a cisgender, white, male perspective. No one can know the true horrors of our experience more than that of those within the community and tell those stories with justice and empathy both behind and in front of the camera.

References

Allen, R. (2007). Hitchcock's Romantic Irony (Film and Culture Series) (Illustrated ed.). Columbia University Press.

Benshoff, H., Jancovich, M., & Schaefer, E. (1997). Monsters in the closet: Homosexuality and the Horror Film (Inside Popular Film). Manchester University Press.

Gardner, C. (2018). Wrong Men, Wrong Women, Wrong Time: Queer Characters in Hitchcock – Flaming Classics. Flaming Classics. http://flamingclassics.com/wrong-men-wrong-women-wrong-time-queer-characters-in-hitchcock/

Leff, L. J., & Simmons, J. (2001). The Dame in the Kimono: Hollywood Censorship and the Production Code from the 1920s to the 1960s. Trafalgar Square.

GENDER REALISATION THROUGH HORROR MOVIES: HOW HORROR MOVIES HELPED ME REALISE I AM NON-BINARY

BERNADETTA F

Content Warning: transphobia

From the very beginning, I wanted this essay to be about my non-binary identity and its relation to horror however, my original idea was going to be focused on awesome depictions of trans and non-binary people in horror. Starting out I didn't know about any positive trans/non-binary characters in horror, and I only got increasingly sad and frustrated about this the more I searched for positive examples. This doesn't mean I didn't find any cool examples—one that has really stuck with me is *The Missing: J.J Macfield and the Island of Memories* (2018)— but I couldn't find enough examples for me to focus my ideas into a positive retrospective on trans and non-binary horror characters. And, yeah, that really did make me sad. It was in this moment of sadness that I came to an important crossroads. I decided that I could either write a manifesto about how desperately we need more trans and non-binary characters in horror, OR I could focus on the very real influence that the women of horror have had on my journey to finding out who exactly I am. I ended up choosing the latter, not because the former didn't have any value, but because I wanted to focus on some trans joy. To make it extremely clear, we DO need more trans and non-binary representation in horror, not just as serial killers or victims—I want a badass non-binary final girl—or SOMETHING, please!

Before we begin properly, I just wanted to say that, although this is a very personal essay filled with all my personal weirdness I developed as a third culture kid growing up in Belgium (and in my earlier years a very limited euro-centric lens regarding horror), I hope that other non-binary people can be inspired to look back and see how important media from their childhood might have shaped them in more ways than they realise. While we may lack proper representation at the moment, nobody can take away what we relate to.

Childhood

Many of my earliest memories are related to horror: the jump-scare at the end of *Friday the 13th* (1980) literally making me feel sick with fear, Chucky coming to life and teaching my first set of naughty words in *Child's Play* (1988), the list could go on and on, with most of these memories being very fond ones. I do have to say though, even though I've always loved horror, I haven't always loved Freddy Krueger—as a child I was absolutely terrified of him. It was originally a promotional still of Robert Englund in full makeup which sent me into a hysterical fear before even seeing him in a film. When I did actually watch *A Nightmare on Elm Street* (1984) for the first time, it kept me awake for almost an entire year. There were many nights where I sat paralysed in my bed convinced that a knife-fingered glove would come up the side of my bed. This was when I was about eight, way too young for that kind of terror. Some years later, when I was about eleven (still way too young), I managed to get the guts to watch the film again, and something wonderful happened this second time around, I felt a true connection with a character on screen for the first time—this character being the wonderfully brave and strong Nancy. Maybe it's just a coincidence (if you believe in such a thing) that the first character that I really related to was female, but I distinctly remember thinking that most male characters in horror movies acted like complete jackasses and just could never imagine responding to a horror movie situation with the weird bravado often depicted on-screen (granted, I grew up with a lot of late '90s and early 2000s horror which is notorious for having really just awful male characters in them). I wanted to be as brave, tough and tender as Nancy—who was all these things even when the worst possible events were happening to her. Memories of Nancy's triumph when confronting her tormentor head-on would stick with me through some really tough times later in life.

On the note of strong female characters that strongly influenced yours truly, I have to mention *Resident Evil* (2002) and *Underworld* (2003). While looking back on them now I probably wouldn't call either of these films "good" (whatever that even means), but damn are they are damn fun. Watching the heroines of these movies kick zombie and/or werewolf/vampire/mutant combinations butt actually gave me my first taste of dysphoria. For some people reading this it might sound like a really weird thing to look back on positively, and it does bring up a lot of bad/uncomfortable feelings, but in a way, looking back on this time in my life, it feels like an epiphany of sorts. Let me explain myself.

The main reason I have seen these films many, MANY times is because of a certain male presence in my life, who to protect his feelings and to not embarrass him, will go unnamed (because I love him very much). This person was very attracted to both Alice (*Resident Evil*) and Selene (*Underworld*). Being an impressionable AMAB child born into an environment where heteronormativity reigned supreme, I assumed that I was also supposed to be attracted to them. So I tried, I really did try, but I just kept on getting weird feelings that I couldn't quite place. I just couldn't help but wonder how great it would be to be able to look and act like these characters, striding down the school corridors in tight-fitting pleather jeans and a long, flowing black coat. Unfortunately, without the proper resources to understand these feelings or anyone in my life with an understanding of what I was going through, I just began to assume I was abnormal. I really felt more like one of the horrible mutants in those films rather than one of the leading ladies. So, for the most part, I pushed down the parts of me that wanted to look feminine and focused more on the goth/metal side of these characters and films—but the powerful femininity of these characters definitely influenced me in the long run. I truly believe that both Mila Jovovich and Kate Beckinsale manage to break the male gaze of their films directors somewhat through their—in my opinion—truly iconic performances. It's true, I experienced a lot of dysmorphia back then, which was probably a net negative for my self-esteem growing up; however, I genuinely don't think I would have been set onto my current path of self-discovery without these characters, and I certainly would not be physically presenting myself in the way that I do now, as a sort of wannabe vampire.

Teenage Years

After having successfully acquired some dysmorphia and a love for pitch-black clothing, I set out into my teenage years. I spent these years (roughly thirteen to seventeen) believing that I was a cis-gay man, and oh boy I spent a lot of effort trying to appear as gay as possible. The only positive representation that I saw of gay teenagers around this time was *Glee* (2009-2015). In my mind, you were either a Blaine or a Kurt, which in retrospect is hilarious because of my obsession with horror. If you want an accurate representation of me from this time, think of a campy, somewhat masculine version of Selene from *Underworld*. My idea of what a gay man is at this point came almost entirely from *Glee*.

I went through a particularly morbid phase in which I was completely obsessed with *Hellraiser* (1987) and alienated quite a few of my peers, insisting that it was the best film ever made. While it may not be the best film ever made, it was still absolutely ground-breaking for its time for its visuals, story and themes. Many people have talked about it as a wonderful piece of LGBTQ+ horror (Deininger, 2020) and some have even viewed the film as a statement against the gender binary and the nuclear family (Sautman, 2019). For me this makes total sense—what scares bigoted cis-people more than the idea of someone not being either a 'biological' man or a 'biological' woman? From the first time I watched the film, I remember being fascinated by the apparent sexlessness and lack of gender of the Cenobites; this had been the first time in my life I even considered there might be actual real-life people who don't think of themselves as being either male or female. I found it extremely interesting how some people really focused and objectified the seemingly female aspects of some Cenobites (the marketing for later *Hellraiser* films being very guilty of this, as well as some of the films themselves). This sentiment was odd to me then and is even more odd to me now. Do the Cenobites give a fuck about where they fit into the gender binary? Given that they are immortal BDSM demons, I think probably not.

Another film that opened up my mind to a lot of ideas was *Frankenstein Created Woman* (1967)—I absolutely adored the Hammer Horror films in my teenage years, especially as they had just enough class to them that I could watch them without getting judged by my parents—but they were still spooky enough to give me a thrill. By the time I got around to watching *Frankenstein Created Woman*, I had thought I knew what to expect from one of these films, but to my surprise, this film is actually quite a thoughtful reflection that challenges the viewers' perceptions around gender. Absolutely mind-blowing stuff, especially when you consider that it was made in the 1960s! I can only imagine the questions or outrage this film would have caused back then. This was the first time I had ever seen a piece of media that put into words the idea of somebody being trapped in a body they did not feel at home in. Before this, I simply just thought I was broken, and I struggled really hard with feeling like I didn't belong anywhere, not even in my own body. Sure, I had heard of trans people, and as mentioned before, had even entertained the idea that it was possible, perhaps, for somebody to be neither male nor female. But I never thought that could apply to me. But luckily this truly weird-ass film from the '60s managed to open up some doors in my mind and got me thinking about myself in a very different way. However, ultimately it would be another film that would inspire me to start experimenting with looking explicitly feminine, rather than just vaguely vampire-like, and of course, it was a horror adjacent film, *Beetlejuice* (1988). Seeing Winona Ryder's Lydia for the first time made me lose my patience with myself and made me decide that I MUST look like that immediately. The resulting experimenting with feminine clothing did truly make me feel euphoric with how I looked for the first time—I finally saw myself as hopefully being able to be as badass as Alice or Selene or as gentle as Nancy, taking inspiration from each one of these characters, who although fictional had left a real, meaningful impact on me. Unfortunately, a bad run-in with an authority figure pushed me backwards in my journey; I'm sure many AMAB trans and non-binary people have heard the classic "I won't have any cross-dressing under my roof" line before. Despite putting up some fierce resistance at first, I ended up forgetting about expressing myself physically for a long time.

Moving to University

As mentioned before, I barely had any frame of reference for what it meant to be not straight, and I certainly had no real idea of what it meant to be trans, except for a few little glimpses here and there. Any idea that I was anything other than a cis man was placed firmly in a box, that was, in turn, pushed to the back of my mind. Fortunately, I would soon rediscover this box once I left home for University. Back in Belgium, I was painfully shy, I could barely even talk to my friends never mind strangers. But once I moved to the North of England to study, a switch flipped in my head. Once arriving in the UK, I gained so much confidence and a proper sense of self. I had forgotten questions around my gender identity and was swept up in a newfound feeling of validation. I found people who really loved the same things that I did, who treated me with kindness and accepted me. I felt momentarily on top of the world. As I settled down, the feelings of dysmorphia began to return. My new surroundings provided kindness and warmth that fought off those unwanted feelings. And that's where *Your Number Is Up* comes into the picture. "What's that?" you're maybe thinking to yourself, what cinematic masterpiece are they talking about? Well unfortunately for you I'm not talking about some sort of obscure horror gem, but rather a pretty mediocre horror short I wrote and directed while studying. As much as I dislike the film, it is important to me. Well, specifically the remake is—yes, I remade the film because I disliked the original version so much. It was while shooting this updated version in my third year of my undergrad degree that I met a non-binary person for the first time.

I've always written all my scripts in a gender-neutral fashion, none of my characters have explicitly been written as male or female. This was actually entirely out of necessity, as whenever I shot a film, I would grab whoever would be willing to be in my weird little films at the time. I could never afford to be picky with who I cast in my films, so I decided to avoid tricky rewrites and just adapt the character to the actor once it had been cast. This is exactly what happened with the remake for *Your Number Is Up*. I put out a general casting all around the University and just cast whoever responded first, as I had left filming until way too late. And boom, it just so happened that one of the people who responded was non-binary. I wish I could say that we adapted the character into being explicitly non-binary, but the cinematographer and I were far too concerned with making the film look nice while also trying to get as much of the film shot in as quick of a time as possible, all while dealing with unusually hot weather in May. It was just the two of us doing cameras, audio, direction, cinematography and catering. It was a bit of a disaster. I did get the opportunity to talk to this actor, and the idea of not being male, nor explicitly female was something that really resonated with me. After this hectic shoot was done, I certainly had a lot to think about. I really wish I could say that meeting this person made me realise that I am non-binary right then and there, but unfortunately for me, this was not the case. However, after this initial meeting, I began to reconsider my approach to writing scripts. I began thinking it might be good to create characters that were intentionally neither male nor female as a CHOICE, rather than through just necessity. With this aim in mind, I began educating myself about non-binary gender identities, and as a by-product of this, I slowly began opening up that aforementioned box. What originally started as a writing tool, soon developed into a new approach on how to view myself and my relation to the gender binary. I felt like I could finally start asking informed and meaningful questions about myself, and even more crucially, I felt like I could start answering them.

After University

Once I finished my undergraduate degree, I signed up to do a master's degree in a different city, taking with me all my newly found thoughts surrounding my gender identity. Unfortunately, around this time dysmorphia really started to creep back in for the first time in a while. A very subtle kind, partially brought on by the new environment I found myself in, the extremely heteronormative, grey and at times extremely dour world of Political and International Studies. I felt that I somewhat needed to look the part and so tried to fit in the best I could with my long hair and wardrobe that mostly consisted of slightly horrifying horror and metal t-shirts. It was honestly stifling. There were many days I wished I could rock up to my European Union Studies seminar rocking the Elvira look, just so I could add some sort of fun into these people's lives. Luckily I had a wonderful support network outside of my studies that really helped me stay sane, and I was lucky enough to be able to regularly indulge myself by watching a cheesy slasher with an awesome scream queen at the helm, be it Jamie Lee Curtis, Heather Langenkamp, Neve Campbell or countless others. These movies gave me a safe haven, where I could retreat after spending the day studying incredibly tough topics like civil wars and British foreign policy.

It was around this time in my life that I met my partner. They love spooky things as much as I do (with the only rule being that zombies are an absolute NO go). Growing up, they did not get to watch all the horror films that I had. Naturally, I felt that this had to change. Over the course of getting to know each other, we made our way slowly through the classics of my childhood—current favourites are *The Texas Chain Saw Massacre* (1974) and *Halloween* (1978). However, all of these films were ones that I'd watched plenty of times before and so didn't really stir up any new emotions or thoughts in me (except for increasing appreciation for these films). What did stir up new, important thoughts inside me was a movie my partner showed me, *The Craft* (1996). I instantly fell in love with the '90s as hell aesthetics and angst— very much on-brand for me. It felt like a Kittie album put on screen. After finishing up the film, I casually mentioned in an off-hand, half-joking manner that I wish I could have looked like the main characters in the film while growing up. My partner responded to this by saying "You could look like that now!." This led to a running joke of me saying "I wish I could look like *insert feminine character here*" and my partner saying "do it." Over the next year and a bit, this joke continued, but in my mind, it

117

became less of a joke and more of a genuine statement. Could I just *"DO IT"*? With this idea becoming more prevalent and dominant in my head, the final push to admit to myself that I am non-binary came about from, unsurprisingly, while I was watching another horror movie. In October 2020 I decided to show my partner *The Witch* (2015). At this point, I had already begun experimenting with gender-neutral pronouns with my partner but was still unsure just WHAT my identity was. I knew I definitely leant more towards femininity than masculinity, but an exact answer was just outside of my grasp, constantly being pushed away from me by an over-active brain and self-doubt. Looking back I was still holding onto a lot of baggage that was holding me back. Something about this cold, Autumn night had set my mind into a self-reflective mood. As I watched Thomasin becoming one with the witches, revelling in her newfound freedom and separating herself from the norms of the society she was bought up in, something clicked. I felt all of this baggage just suddenly drop, any uncertainties I had burned away and I felt lighter, almost like I could fly away like Thomasin, and I felt the euphoric moment of realising that I am indeed non-binary.

A Final Reflection (For the Moment)

It might seem hackneyed or cliché to some, but I really don't think I would have been able to admit who I am without the horror movies that I grew up with. Without the exploration of the genre I engaged in as I grew up. Without the inspiration to make my own questionable horror movies. There were other elements to my journey, and I truly would not have made it this far without all the wonderful, beautiful people I know, but watching and thinking about horror has helped me understand so many things about myself, and that's the truth.

References

Deininger, K. (2020). *Hellraiser: Why Clive Barker's Movie Has Become A Queer Horror Classic.* [online] ScreenRant. Available at: https://screenrant.com/hellraiser-clive-bark er-movie-queer-horror-classic-reason/

Sautman, M. (2020). *Domestic Bodies in Hell: The Significance of Gendered Embodi ment in Clive Barker's Hellraiser.* Body Studies, 2(7), 66–78.

THE LOVE OF MY LIFE

KRISTEN

What does horror mean to you? Some say movies, some say it is a celebration of Halloween, some say it is a way of life. Horror can be defined in different ways, but to me is horror is my escape, my true love, and my passion. For me, horror and mental health go hand in hand. Mental health is important to me because I, myself, have my own struggles which I know other people do as well. A lot of people in the horror community have talked to me about the fact that horror has helped them with their mental state, saying "horror helps bring fears to the surface, helping you release struggle instead of internalizing it."

Mental health and representation can also go hand in hand because you can relate to an experience, what if someone just like you were on the big screen? It can really pull you into the story and make you feel more connected to that character. I have felt this particular connection with the movies *Midsommar* and *What Keeps You Alive* as both films have given me help to release a past traumatic experience and, as a lesbian, feel seen. Though I have related to both films, I would love to see a more accurate representation of LGBTQ+ people in the horror genre. Whilst horror does not have the best history of representation of these characters, I feel that we are moving towards a new direction, creating a new history for the future.

Growing up religious, my parents did not want horror movies in the household thinking it would bring in unwanted guests. I was allowed to watch movies like *Scooby-Doo* and cartoons; honestly when I was younger the thought of horror movies scared me. Growing up, I remember that my Dad and I shared a passion for BigFoot, and we always watched all the new documentaries together. At the age of eleven, my dad had recorded a new documentary for us to watch called *Abominable*, however, this movie was not a documentary as we thought it was. This was my first introduction into the world of horror. I remember seeing the Yeti pull a woman down through the ceiling and proceed to rip her throat off. This made me absolutely sick to my stomach and my mother started to scream at my father to, " TURN IT OFF!!". For two weeks after seeing this film, I slept with a nightlight on in my room because I thought the Yeti was coming for me.

These movies terrified me which is kind of funny to look back on now. Even though horror movies were not quite my forte, my mom LOVED true crime shows and documentaries. *Dateline, 20/20, Snapped, Forensic Files* were just a few of the shows she watched with me on a regular basis. For as long as I can remember, I have loved true crime and I have always considered it a part of horror. Even to this day they are still a comfort watch for me. When I was sixteen years old, I had a best friend who was super into horror films. She would light up talking about them. In this moment, I realized that this beaming feeling was something I also wanted to experience in my life. Since she recognized my desire to explore the world of horror she suggested I start with *The Grudge*. It scared me to death, and I did not sleep for a week. For some reason though, I wanted more. I dove in heavily on the classics, such as *Halloween, A Nightmare on Elm Street, Child's Play,* and even *Scream. Scream* was the one that did it. To me it was like watching an adult version of *Scooby-Doo,* which like I said was a huge part of my childhood. It was then I truly loved the genre, but it was not until recently where I fell in love with it.

Midsommar was when I fell. This movie helped me release a traumatic experience in my past. I went to the theater not even sure of what I was expecting, but I walked out with a burden lifted off my shoulders. It was like a release and a therapy session I did not know I truly needed. When I was 17, I remember a past relationship where my boyfriend spent a couple years gaslighting me, in turn making me feel like the bad guy in the relationship. There were times where I was blamed for things that I did not feel like were my fault such as birthdays or events. In the film when Dani tells Pelle that she forgot to remind Christian that it was her birthday and thus it was her fault he forgot, this resonated with me. This film really highlights the toxic parts of a relationship between Dani and Christian. When Pelle asks Dani if she felt held, I knew how she felt. I felt like I was reliving that moment with her and it was hard to watch. We witness Dani experience a euphoric, cleansing moment where she chooses to watch Christian burn. It was that exact moment for Dani when she realized she could escape from Christian and find true freedom. The way this part of the film was portrayed was exactly what I needed to release this toxic ex of mine, and I will forever and always thank Ari Aster for that. I felt seen and understood in that movie and that is why I truly fell in absolute love with the genre. *Midsommar* inspired me to get my first horror-themed tattoo. Inspired by the ending of the film where Christian was being burned alive in the sacred building. I got an image of that building burning on my hand to symbolize the cleansing and release of that past trauma. I wanted to include the Elder Futhark runes on my fingers that meant something to me as well, so I looked up what they meant and picked the ones that resonated with me the most (Fehu, Sowilo, Algiz, Dagaz, and Othala). I am sure that others have experienced their own horror films where they have released a terrible situation, or it has helped them release a horrible memory from their past. Horror is very much a comfort for me, I cannot tell you how many times I have had a bad day and just wanted to cuddle up and watch a horror movie. When I watch a horror film it is like my brain realizing things could be worse so in that aspect it gives me comfort. Horror honestly keeps us sane, it helps us release the anger, the frustration, the sadness, whatever feeling we have in that moment. Just like Wes Craven said, "Horror doesn't create fear, it releases it."

As much as *Midsommar* made me feel seen, it helped with some experiences and aspects of my own mental health journey. There are many benefits to being seen through the horror genre and how representation can help everyone. There are many experiences that I can relate to, but seeing someone that has the same sexual orientation as me can make someone feel even more represented. As a lesbian, one aspect of films that I find degrading in the depiction of lesbian relationships is the oversexualization of the relationship, usually manifested through sex scenes that are not very tastefully done. The movie *What Keeps You Alive* directed by Colin Minihan is a true gem. The film shows Jackie and Jules, a regular lesbian couple, and does not make a big deal about it at all. Even when there is a sex scene, it is not full nudity and is tastefully done. They have regular struggles just like any other couple. They even have dinner with their friends that are straight and there is nothing off about it. It is refreshing to see that being normalized and I applaud that movie for doing so. Seeing this representation, makes me feel like being in a same sex relationship is 100% normalized just like any straight relationship is. The normal relationships seen on camera were primarily heterosexual, so this day and age it is nice to see the new normal. The more we see the LGBTQ+ representation, the more normalized it will become. Personally, I feel like we have a long way to go, but I have noticed changes are starting to form. I commend the creators and writers who are already showing us this change. We truly appreciate you!

So, what is horror to you? How do you feel you are being represented in the genre? What movies have made you feel seen or release a past traumatic event? *Midsommar* and *What Keeps You Alive* did a lot for me, and I hope that they touched other lives as well. If not those movies, then I hope you have that one horror movie that made you fall in love with the genre because of it. One day I hope that the representation in the LGBTQ community will be so normal that you will not even have to say, "Oh! Look there is a gay character in this" or "Oh yeah they are gay," and one day just say, "they are in a relationship and that is cool." The horror community is such a loving, welcoming one and I have met some absolute gems that I will know for the rest of my life. A family I can call home that helps keep me sane. I will always be grateful to horror creators of all kinds for what they do. Thank you for helping me get here. Thank you for all the love.

REBIRTH OF BLACK HORROR CINEMA: HORROR FANDOM THROUGH THE BLACK LENS

KYASIA FIELDS

I can remember moving to Texas from Louisiana in 2003 and being petrified when hearing stories of *The Texas Chainsaw Massacre*. Everyone in school claimed it was based on true events. I just couldn't conjure the idea that my mother would move me to this state where I could potentially fall victim to a chainsaw slinging cannibal (of course in the 5th grade I wasn't aware that the film was NOT based on true events but loosely based on the Wisconsin Serial Killer Ed Gein). Moved by the story, I began to obsess and during a free-write assignment in Mrs Huffine's class, I poured my feelings and thoughts on this terrible series of events. I got an A, but I never knew at that moment I was planting a seed for my destiny. Growing up I was truly afraid of Halloween and all things spooky. From the ages of four to eight, I wouldn't step foot in a Walmart or other store during the month of October. Granted, I did watch a few cult classics like *Deep Blue Sea* (1999) (which brings great nostalgia of my grandmother and her home-cooked meals) and *Halloween Resurrection* (2002) growing up, but having rappers like LL Cool J and Busta Rhymes in these films granted a sense of excitement and comfort because I liked their music and they were familiar to me. Watching films like those helped me shed my fear and grow fonder of the genre. I can vividly remember watching *Final Destination* at the age of six with my aunt and uncle (who were huge horror fans) and not being able to use the restroom by myself for weeks because of Tod's shower death scene. I just knew that as soon as I was left alone in the shower that I too would fall to the same demise. Though I was young, the idea that you couldn't see the killer and it was death itself did not sit right with me—that movie changed my life and how I view horror movies.

Middle and high school were a difficult time as a horror fan due to my family life and upbringing being very religious. We were not allowed to participate in any Fall activities. I can recall sneaking Stephen King novels in my room and scaring myself to death while reading *IT* (1986) and *Nightmares & Dreamscapes* (1993). Around my senior year of high school I stopped caring what others thought of my fandom and slowly grew more outward with my love for the genre. My fondest memory during that time of my life was spending my Saturdays when I wasn't working locked in my room watching horror films on the SyFy channel. It introduced me to more in-depth films and characters in the genre (and also a few of my guilty pleasures like *Wrong Turn* (2003) and *Rest Stop* (2006). Now being a non-binary horror loving fanatic I realized that I wasn't as comfortable being my authentic self in range of my fandom until college. I met a guy after a college party whom I grew close with after discovering his outward passion for the genre. This was the first person I met around my age that loved horror as much as I did and looked like me. His room was decked in cool posters and paraphernalia and had huge tattoos of iconic characters and monsters. We worked together on our campus's haunted house and countless creative projects. By this time in my life, I had established myself as a self-taught special effects artist, and he was a photographer—it worked so well with all of the creepy ideas and brainstorming. Befriending and watching him being his authentic self as a horror movie loving Black man truly inspired me. I started posting more about my favorite films on social media and reading more academic based horror studies books. Most of my work in undergrad consisted of me criticizing my favorite films or finding social critiques in cult classics. A few of my professors, including Dr. Toniesha Taylor (a communications professor who was deathly afraid of reading my critiques), noticed my growing interest and guided me into the realm of Black horror academia, where I was introduced to brilliant scholars like Dr. Kinitra Brooks, Tananarive Due, Dr. Robin Means Coleman and many others.

Lost in Representation

As I began to dive deeper into the constructs and tropes of the genre I was taken aback by the lack of representation for Black, queer, and disabled persons in films. Most depictions of Blacks in the genre consist of overlooked side characters that are only there to aid the advancement of the survival of others (i.e. the side character who gives the final girl and her dumb boyfriend clues to kill the killer), the hypermasculine man who usual falls to their demise because of their pride (Lewis Roneros character in *Final Destination 3* (2006) played by Texas Battle), the comedic relief who usually gets killed off due to recklessness, and the all time "favorite," the insignificant character who is killed within the first act of the film with no background, history or humanity, just a body (Darick The Dockhand in *I Still Know What You Did Last Summer* (1998) played by Benjamin Brown). We were rarely the "final girls" or lasting characters with fulfilling backstories and purpose towards our survival in said film.

Two of my earliest memories of "final girls" were Lori Campbell (played by Monica Keena) in *Freddy V Jason* (2003) and Julie James (played by Jennifer Love-Hewitt) in *I Still Know What You Did Last Summer* (1998). They fit the trope, beautiful, white, virgin women, screaming their way out of harm's way—usually with oblivious boyfriends and daddy issues. They were always saved and they always survived. I wanted to be the final girl. In both films, these characters had Black female best friends who were outspoken, overprotective of their white counterparts while simultaneously trying to hook them up with the nearest "nice guy," smart, and it was always implied that they were sexually active (which we know is broken rule number one of being murdered in a slasher film.) They always seem to bring a grounding and practicality to the final girl, this sense of reality and real perspective. We have Karla Wilson (played by Pop Singer Brandy Norwood) in *I Still Know What You Did Last Summer* (1998) and Kia Waterson (played by Destiny's Child's Kelly Rowland) in *Freddy vs, Jason* (2003). Kia played in the trope of the "mean girl" with the nerdy character Charlie Linderman (played by Chris Marquette) as her main target. Her character was very controversial with a homophobic slur being used in interacting with Jason Voorhees before her death. It was interesting to see that her death was the final death of Jason's in the film, being that generally Black characters tend to die within the first 20-30 minutes. Karla Wilson was on the other end of the spectrum of representation. She was lovable and charismatic. You can tell that she genuinely cared about Julie and wanted her to feel comfortable and relax during a traumatic time. She was the anti-final girl. You have a Black, outspoken, sexually active woman who didn't go out without a fight and came out on the other side with Julie. I loved Karla. I wanted to be Karla. Karla survives.

Cinematic Shifts

Throughout horror history there have been few films that broke through barriers in proper storytelling and representation of Blacks in cinema, from the revenge filled semi-progressive Blacksploitation films like *Blacula* (1972), *Ganja & Hess* (1973), and *Sugar Hill* (1974) to '90s fan favorites like *Tales from the Hood* (1995), *Candyman* (1992), and Wes Craven's *The People Under The Stairs* (1991). The start of the new millennium saw a genre shift from slashers and cult classic killers to post 9/11 motiveless violence with the likes of *Saw* (2004) and *Hostel* (2005), paranormal universes with *Insidious* (2010) and *The Conjuring* (2013), and found footage post-apocalyptic films like *Cloverfield* (2008), *Paranormal Activity* (2007) and *Quarantine* (2008). The end of the 2010s created a resurgence of avant garde horror films that made you think, with Ari Aster's 2018 slow burn film *Hereditary* and Jordan Peele's *Get Out* (2017).

Rebirth of Black Horror Cinema

My initial reaction to watching the trailer for *Get Out* was, "wow this looks interesting, did Jordan Peele really come up with this?", that being in conjunction with my only knowledge of Peele's work as comedy with his Comedy Central show *Key & Peele*. I was impressed but not enough to run to the theatre during the opening weekend to watch the film. It wasn't until my parents—who are tough critics—saw the film and raved over it that I was sold. I ran to the theatre to see it. My entire outlook on the lengths horror could go changed. During that time I was a sponge soaking up as much social criticism as possible to help push me through my last year of college (for the sake of writing content), and establishing myself as a Black horror academic. I had never seen so much of myself in a film—a horror film at that.

I always say when asked about *Get Out*, that for most viewers it is simply a well put together horror film that breaks down the concept of the liberal racist: the prejudices that live beyond white hoods in this country. For most Black Americans *Get Out* can be described as a documentary, showing the collective fear of being a black face in a white space. A haunting depiction of how a "common" interaction (i.e. a Black man going to visit his white girlfriend's parents for the first time) can be ruled in hatred. You see the humanity in Chris's character. His fears, how he has to be in a constant state of hyper-awareness of his Blackness.

I knew I wanted to continue my studies discussing Black representation in horror (or the lack thereof), but after watching such a profound film such as *Get Out* and witnessing the conversation and impact it had in the community, I knew I wanted to do more.

Finding Community

The summer of 2020 stirred a whirlwind of emotions, with the emergence of the COVID-19 virus, unexpected nationwide quarantine, and wrongful death of George Floyd at the hands of law enforcement. Protestors rushed the streets across the nation in alliance with the BLACKLIVESMATTER movement to show support in getting proper justice served for Floyd's death and overall police reform. When social issues arise, capitalists tend to create the illusion that major corporations and businesses care and empathize with social issues (but instead use that as a means to create emotional relationships with consumers, therefore boosting their products and advertisement). The summer consisted of said companies highlighting Black faces to "show solidarity" with the Black Community and protestors. My social media feed was suddenly filled with talented Black horror content creators, fans, and enthusiasts, myself included. I had never seen so many beautiful Black faces before in the horror community. So much passion and fandom. Granted, when I attended major horror conventions in the country I could count on both hands how many people were walking around that looked like myself. Initially, I was inspired to create a platform for Black horror news—with the renaissance of new horror films, I figured I would have enough content to get me through for awhile—but after coming across so many talented creatives I knew I wanted to do more. Tell the story of how these creators fell in love with the genre like I did. What sparked their creativity? What keeps them going? I felt as if I found my purpose in the community besides turning people into monsters with my makeup effects. Though 2020 was a year filled with tragedy and uncertainty, horror found a community, and KyFx Horror Group was born. A multimedia platform supporting inclusion within the horror genre while accentuating the importance of Black horror content creators. A space to tell the story of "the other," those who are underrepresented in the genre—to question the tropes presented in film. Why is it that sexually active people die in comparison to "the virgin"? Why aren't there more disabled or queer survivors? Why are those in rural areas seen as incestuous/cannabalistic in comparison to those who live in urban areas?

I created a website highlighting Black, Indigenous, Persons of Color, LGBTQIA+, and disabled horror fans with my KyFx Content Creature Features, a detailed transcribed interview discussing the backgrounds and forefronts of these creators while pushing their current projects. I curated lists of these creators to follow on social media and broadcasted as much Black horror media content as I could. During each interview, I hear the passions in their voices and light in their stories.

You Can't Police Our Horrors

With the growth and recognition of KyFx Horror Group, came a following on social media from many facets of fans. The KyFx Horror Group Instagram page grew to have over one thousand followers after six months of being established. I was being asked to guest star on podcast episodes and panels discussing the importance of inclusion and Black horror. It was a bit overwhelming at times because I felt like the weight of the world was on my shoulders to pump out as much content as possible to stay relevant. When I made KyFx Horror Group, it was intended to be a safe space. No hatred, judgement, just horror and fun. With the unity and support of horror fans from all walks of life, I assumed KyFX was untouchable, safe from hatred and biased commentary, especially with the social climate of the prior summer. It was brought to my attention via Twitter that a few BIPOC creators and platforms had been subject to racial injustice and gatekeeping. I was no stranger to online gatekeeping of horror . Non-Black fans create criteria of what films to watch to be considered a "real horror fan," most not including Black horror classics. If you haven't seen such movies, you aren't considered a "true fan." It was also evident that there still was a divide in the community after major horror broadcasting companies sided with their Black creators and an oversaturation of negative, racist comments were highlighted, and even some fans saying that they will no longer support said companies because they were acknowledged.

KyFx Horror group faced its own prejudices when non-Black fans made comments discrediting the vision and mission of the platform. While making the weekly "SUPPORT BLACK HORROR" post on social media as a reminder, a disgruntled follower commented, "what about all horror, why does it have to be black versus white." I didn't get an opportunity to truly digest the comment before my colleagues came in to set the record straight with said follower. My intention with the post wasn't to discredit any other demographic of horror fans, it was to highlight a demographic that historically has been cast aside, overlooked, and not given the opportunity to fight for life on and off film. KyFx Horror Group is a space for the overlooked, for BLACK HORROR. It's common for non-Black fans to come into Black spaces to dictate how we enjoy and express our fandom. We created these spaces because historically we were not included in theirs. African Americans have been policed throughout the duration of our existence in this country from how we should experience daily life, to how we react to the many injustices protected onto us but we can not be policed for our horrors. How disheartening is it to see the disgust from the general fanbase when someone is in alliance with you. Why is it when a podcast with a Black and Queer host has a name similar to another podcast that has a white host, that host feels entitled to confront the other podcast demanding with gaslighting and hateful messaging that they change their name, a name that comes from a popular film in the genre. Why didn't that podcast host confront the other hundreds of other platforms and social media pages with the same name or one similar? Horror belongs to all of us.

Thank You, Horror

Through progression and awareness, horror is growing to be a genre for everyone, a beautifully haunting reflection of its fans. Though the journey to finding my passion and purpose in the genre wasn't linear, my love for horror never changed. From the times I covered my eyes from fear in the theatre as a child watching Flight 180 blow up in mid-air, to dedicating my life's work so fans who look like me (or don't) feel seen and heard, a tool for justice and un-derstanding. Historically, we've seen the true nature of society through horror films, the fears, the prejudices, and the darkness, but for me and many others horror is a light, a way of expression and community, the gratitude is infinite. Thank you, Horror.

DON'T DREAM IT, DO IT: OUR JOURNEY TO CREATING A QUEER HORROR FILM FESTIVAL

ELECIA PAGE AND SAM WHITAKER

Queer folk have long been identified – and found self-identification – with monstrosity on screen, from the social exclusion of creatures such as vampires to queer-coded villains like Norman Bates to the openly gender-queer Dr. Frank N Furter. We know how important this visible representation is for the queer community. Queerness has existed in horror films for as long as horror films have been made. We only need to look back at James Whale's *The Old Dark House* (1932) and *The Bride of Frankenstein* (1935) to see a queer director making movies about isolation, desire, and the rejection of social norms. However, in 1934 The Motion Picture Production Code, otherwise known as The Hays Code, made it difficult to share openly queer stories. The code banned representations of homosexuality on screen and imposed other restrictions under the guise of 'morality'. The code was lifted in 1968 but still lingers on in the social subconscious.

Whilst the removal of The Hays Code has led to more diverse and explicitly queer characters and story lines, there are signs that the legacy of the code continues to affect mainstream cinema through the promotion of white patriarchal ideals. An example of this can be seen in *Jennifer's Body* (Kusama, 2009), an overtly feminist and queer film which at the time of its release was misunderstood by critics. Instead of focusing on the content and merit of the filmmaking, critics were more focused on the appearance and sexuality of the titular character played by Megan Fox. This critical reception undermined the queerness of Jennifer and reframed her character to exist purely for the consumption of the male gaze.

From banning the 'promotion' of homosexuality to erasing the queerness of

130

characters, queer stories have been heavily suppressed over the years. This is why we think it is imperative to create the opportunity and the space for queer people to express themselves and their stories through the medium of film. We're reflecting here on our personal relationships with horror films and the journey that led us to start Out For Blood, a queer horror film festival based in Cambridgeshire U.K.

Elecia and a collection of ghost stories

As a child, I collected ghost stories. The scarier, the better. The credit for this peculiar hobby belongs to my mother, who once joyfully told me the ghastly folk history of a local spring known as Emma's Well, effectively starting up my quest to devour any spooky tale I could track down.

My parents divorced when I was a baby, and I grew up mostly with my mum and four younger siblings in a three-bedroom terraced council house. My mum worked as a childminder during the day and shelf-stacked in a supermarket throughout the night. Our house was small and chaotic, so mum took us out on trips as often as possible so that we wouldn't run up the walls or draw on things we shouldn't. Emma's Well, near my childhood home in Hertfordshire U.K., was one of my favourite places to explore.

The story goes like this: a long time ago, a little girl — who was about my age when I first heard this tale — was playing by the well and tragically fell in. When her body was recovered, the cause of death was determined to be drowning, which is a fairly normal conclusion to come to given the location... Except the well was bone dry when she was found. Local legend said if you walk all the way around the well and say her name, the ghostly figure of Emma would appear and beckon you to the well. Sort of like a creepy child version of Bloody Mary. I can honestly say I tried summoning Emma many times with my siblings — we would wait anxiously with baited breath, to absolutely no avail. This minor setback did not stop our spectral pursuit each time we visited, though.

That is what horror is for me: A story shared, passing through different voices, eras, and changing a little bit with each retelling. Feeling a bubbling mix of tension and excitement all squeezed together. The apprehension, the wait for something to happen.

As Emma's no-show continued, my collection of ghost stories did not give me the payoff I was expecting. Luckily, I found horror movies. I watched *Carrie*

(De Palma, 1976) and *The Rocky Horror Picture Show* (Sharman, 1975) over and over again with my mum, and slashers and zombie flicks with my dad. I felt safe watching with my parents, and I loved to share all of the gory details with my friends afterwards. My best friends and I rented some of my favourites at our local corner shop for sleepovers. This was the early 2000s after all. Our newsagent didn't care how old we were as long as we spent the little pocket money we had on sweets to go with whatever film we picked. We would wait until late at night, turn the volume down low so we wouldn't get caught and hold our hands over each other's mouths to stop ourselves from shrieking.

My parents didn't care what I watched — until they saw *The Descent* (Marshall, 2005) at the cinema and told me that I was under no circumstances allowed to watch it. What was I supposed to do? My dad — who isn't afraid of anything — jumped in the theatre watching it. I had to see it! I was 13 when the DVD was released, and as soon as it was available in our shop, I rented it with my friends and smuggled it back to my room under my hoodie. *The Descent* has an unexpected shock near the beginning, but after that, it burns slowly. I had never seen a horror movie with an all-female cast before, and the plot felt authentically written and well-acted. It didn't feel like the scare-by-number films we usually watched. None of us knew what to expect, so the reveal had us screeching and covering our eyes. We turned the light back on and held hands. It was the perfect moment, the building horror culminating in the surprise twist that I so longed for.

I was hooked on horror films. I wasn't picky, but I've always enjoyed the Final Girl trope. As a white cis woman, I could find myself reflected in most horror films, regardless of whether the representation was positive or negative. I re-watched my favourites over and over, looking up to Ellen Ripley in *Alien* (Scott, 1979) and Nancy Thompson in *A Nightmare on Elm Street* (Craven, 1984) until I came out and asked myself the age-old queer question: do I want to be this person or do I fancy them?

As an adult, embracing my identity as a queer woman completely changed my perspective of the horror I loved. I went to see a live showing of Rocky Horror with my mum, and afterwards felt confused by the ending. Who is the antagonist? Is it Dr. Frank N Furter, a queer polyamorous trans person who wants to build the perfect man? Brad and Janet, who experience a sexual awakening, separate from their society-approved hetero relationship? Am I a bad queer person for enjoying a movie where the queer people die? My grown-up (and mostly heterosexual) friends did not watch horror movies. They were generally bemused, but bored if I brought up an in-depth analysis of films they had not seen and had little interest in watching with me. I craved the community I had as a young person, watching scary films with my friends. Except this time, I wanted to see different stories. I wanted to see stories about LGBTQIA+ people who survive until the end. I wanted all types of characters; good, bad, and in between. I wanted people to talk about this with who would be excited with me and share their favourite films and characters.

I wasn't sure where to start - and then I met Sam. Sam was the president of the Feminist Society at the university we were both studying at, and we immediately bonded over issues we were passionate about. We worked together on various campaigns and eventually started dating. Horror movies have always been a date night staple for us, so it was no surprise that we would eventually end up running a queer horror film festival.

Sam and a Fear of Everything

I was a late bloomer when it comes to horror. You see, I grew up in a pretty strict Mormon family, and I was terrified of going to Hell. It might sound pretty far-fetched, but I had many legitimate reasons for worrying about going to Hell; I didn't identify with my assigned female gender and I was hopelessly in love with women. I was very aware of how I identified as a kid. It wasn't until I asked my mum one day after school, "Would God be angry if a girl loved another girl?" that I realised the soul-crushing truth: my family and my religion would not ac-cept me for who I am. So, I went back into the closet to hide who I was amongst the monsters which lurked in there.

As with many religions, we believed in the concept of Good vs Evil. We believed there were evil actions, evil people and evil things. We believed anyone could be corrupted or influenced by evil and if we fell prey to evil, we would spend eternity being punished in the most painful and humiliating ways. Think of the hellscape in *Hellbound: Hellraiser 2* (Randell, 1988), add some boiling lava and you've basically got what I imagined Hell would be like. Therein lies the reason I was such a late bloomer when it comes to horror. Like my religion, horror often deals with the concept of Good vs Evil. Films like *Hellraiser* (Barker, 1987) would literally show images of creatures and worlds from my deepest darkest nightmares – worlds and creatures I thought I would experience if I embraced my true self.

It's interesting looking back on Clive Barker's work now, knowing he is an openly gay man; it helps me identify with his writing and films on a deeper level. Perhaps Barker had similar fears about embracing his own queerness or wanted to talk about the ways mainstream society portrays the queer community as something evil and sinful. Perhaps Barker was inviting queer folk to look at his work and his monsters and asking us to love ourselves and embrace our queerness even when mainstream society wants to call us evil. I wasn't always so willing to have my soul torn apart by Cenobites. Without knowing the language to explore these ideas as a child, something deep down in me knew there was an inherent queerness in horror that felt dangerous.

The first time I collided with my fears of Hell and simultaneously felt immense joy, was when a friend of mine introduced me to *The Rocky Horror Picture Show*. I was already a big fan of musicals, so I was willing to trust my friend. I remember feeling intense, tremendous shame when Sweet Transvestite kicked in. It was as if someone had read my most private thoughts and was releasing them into the world. The scene suddenly made me very aware that living outside of what was expected from your gender wasn't a new concept to the world. This was the first time I really felt represented by a character on screen but I couldn't tell if the character was being celebrated or if they were a joke. I was also very aware of how sexual the film was and how it celebrated the macabre – not exactly things which my church encouraged. My younger self believed just by watching this film, I was committing an evil act and I would be punished for it. Even though it brought me great joy to know there were people like that out there, I couldn't enjoy it and I had to reject it. This was the part of myself I thought I would always have to hide away in that monster-infested closet. Little did I know then that one day I would be so inspired by the opening song 'Science Fiction Double Feature' and the legendary community experience of watching the show, I would want to start a queer horror film festival to encourage the same community viewing.

In my early teens, I was outed to my parents. As expected, being outed caused a great deal of pain between myself and my parents, and after all of the heartache, I realised I had nothing more to be scared of. According to the teachings in my church, I was going to Hell for who I am, so why not embrace it and start enjoying all the things I had previously been scared of.

Elecia and Sam and the Creation of Out For Blood

As queer folk, we grew up feeling different from our heterosexual friends and family around us. We both went to school when Section 28, which criminalised the 'promotion' of homosexuality, was still in effect in England. There was no support available for young people questioning their sexuality or gender identity. Even after Section 28 was repealed, it took years for schools to include LGBTQIA+ History and safe sex education in the curriculum. Exploring our queer identity as young people often felt taboo and shameful. Is it any surprise that we gravitated towards horror? Our favourite childhood movie, *The Addams Family* (Sonnenfeld, 1991) features a family who aren't all blood relatives and celebrates spooky weirdness and living authentically. The drive to rebel against societal norms to find the true inner self is a huge part of the genre, especially in coming of age horror. When we were teenagers and trying to fit in, films like *The Craft* (Fleming, 1996) and *Ginger Snaps* (Fawcett, 2001) explored complex teenage relationships. They showed us that the grass wasn't always greener on the other side, whilst giving us a fix of supernatural scares and body horror. To us, the popular kids in teen screams represented cishet society. When our protagonists finally learned they were better off as their true selves, we felt reflected in our own narrative of self-acceptance away from societal norms.

Horror is a perfect vehicle to explore complex societal themes through allegory, and this was why Sam decided to use horror in their own film work. One of Sam's films was selected by the Final Girls Berlin Film Festival in 2017. At the festival, Sam was told by the organisers that theirs was the only queer film submitted that year. This inspired Sam to create a similar DIY film festival in the UK for queer horror and Out For Blood was born.

When Sam set out to create Out For Blood, they kept in mind the legendary cult following and live audiences that revelled in the joy of Rocky Horror. Sam wanted to create a space where people could come together and feel safe being themselves amongst an audience of like-minded strangers. The festival itself consisted of short horror films either made by queer people or showcasing queer themes. We rigorously watched and examined the films ahead of each festival with a panel of volunteers to ensure the films meet our expectations, both in quality and accessibility. Where some of the films inevitably have themes that may be uncomfortable for some audience members, we take extensive notes when judging the films to create content warnings.

Over the years, there have been things that we have learned, improved, and continue to work on. One of our key takeaways is that not all horror films are born equal. Some of the best films we have shown have had little to no budgets and been made by small teams. It's important to us to highlight not only films with big budgets and visual effects, but more humble films with profound messages.

Something else which has become increasingly important is understanding our limitations of choosing films that are representative of all identities. Before every festival, we put out a call for new volunteers and try to recruit a diverse range of people. When it comes to the judging process, it is critical to recognise some films are made for specific audiences. Therefore, not everyone on our judging panels will necessarily resonate with a film. This means we sometimes select films that were not unanimously popular amongst the entire judging panel, but were good films that represent a diverse group of people on the panel.

Out For Blood has been screening queer horror films for three years so far, and in that time we have met horror fans from all walks of life, as well as filmmakers from across the globe. To ensure that the festival remains a community event, we end the festival with an audience vote for best film. Our first winner in 2018 was *The Quiet Room* directed by Sam Wineman which features a possessive demon who stalks hospital patients. The winner in 2019, *I-RIS* directed by Leila Garrison, follows a girl whose futuristic eye implants cause her trauma to manifest visually. 2020's film festival was hosted online due to the Covid-19 pandemic, and our audience voted *Polter*, directed by Álvaro Vicario, as the winner. *Polter* is a Spanish language comedy horror about a man who needs to discover the source of a paranormal event in his home. We aim to showcase a spread of films from the genre, including ghostly hauntings, teen werewolves, bloodthirsty vampires, and sinister serial killers. We love showing films that subvert our expectations and the conventions of the genre, and we delight in hearing the audience express fear and excitement by gasps, shouts and applause when they connect with the films.

Running a DIY film festival is a huge undertaking, and we are lucky to have the support from our volunteers and the community around us. We are excited to see queer horror fans talking about the genre, creating podcasts, writing essays, and making movies. Horror has always been queer. Queer folk often see themselves reflected in horror, and we hope that we can continue to promote thoughtful and creative queer horror narratives through more community events like Out For Blood.

BODIES, BLOOD, AND BINARIES: DEVELOPING THE TRANS GAZE IN HORROR CINEMA

JENNI HOLTZ

Films are not only a form of widespread and accessible entertainment—they are a reflection of culture and a site of knowledge production. Sigmund Freud and Laura Mulvey describe the love of watching as "scopophilia," or the phenomenon of pleasure gained from looking. When people watch films, even ones that may be frightening like horror films, they can experience pleasure and gain knowledge. Since a majority of films are made by and marketed for a white, cisgender, able-bodied, heterosexual audience, they are catered to people who fit those descriptions. People who do not fit the target demographic have to relate differently to cinema; they watch with an oppositional gaze, as bell hooks described it. The ever-expanding transgender community needs an oppositional trans gaze which specifically examines the damaging portrayal of trans women in horror film using gaze theory, abjection theory, and transgender theory.

The act of watching a movie has been the subject of numerous feminist film critiques, including those by Mulvey and hooks. Mulvey's pivotal essay "Visual Pleasure and Narrative Cinema" explains the male gaze, or the way films are made by men and encourage viewers to gaze upon women in an objectifying manner. Her explanation of the male gaze is a starting point for much of the other film theory about gazing. bell hooks expands Mulvey's theory by describing the experience of the Black female spectator and the power of gazing. She writes that Black female spectators are "Afraid to look, but fascinated by the gaze" because there "is power in looking" (hooks 115). hooks' theory explains how Black women's critical viewing of film is powerful in two ways. First, their critique of mainstream cinema is informed by their more distant relationship to manhood and white womanhood. Second, Black women gain power through gazing because they are able to forge their own space as the center of the story based on how they relate themselves to the story. Putting theory into action, hooks' critique grows into an oppositional gaze that involves actively interrogating white, heterosexual, male-focused films. Another important point hooks makes is that it is possible to enjoy films even if one does not identify directly with them. She explains that even when one views film critically with an oppositional gaze, one may still connect to the emotions, relationships, and character arcs presented. So, looking may still be pleasurable, but critical consciousness is essential. Though Mulvey and hooks explain gazing in terms of sexism, racism, and misogynoir, they do not address how transgender people are able to view film, especially not trans people who identify outside of the binary gender system.

Like Black women's oppositional gaze hooks theorized, trans people still identify with and are affected by films even though they do not directly represent them most of the time. Trans characters are infrequently represented in film, which is reflective of societal attitudes towards transgender people. Thus, when trans people are represented poorly in media, the inaccurate representations shape viewers' idea of what trans people are like. Nonbinary people are represented even less, so the way they gaze at film is of particular interest. Mulvey writes, "in a world ordered by sexual imbalance, pleasure in looking has been split between active/male and passive/female. The determining male gaze projects its fantasy onto the female figure, which is styled accordingly" (19). So, how would someone who does not identify as male or female gaze? What would a film made by a nonbinary director look like? Questions like these are at the forefront of my mind when consuming media as a nonbinary person, existing outside of, between, and around the socially constructed binary gender system. Cisgender and binary transgender people can benefit from asking themselves these questions, too, so they realize the severe lack of nonbinary representation in film and larger society.

There is not nearly enough film theory discussing the transgender experience. Even drawing from transgender theory, there is a tendency to stick to the binary gender system and to minimize identities that fall between and outside of the gender binary. For example, in Susan Stryker's second edition of her book *Transgender History* (2017), she discusses the experiences of trans people in ways that are that are incongruent to the lived experience of nonbinary people. When defining nonbinary and genderqueer identities, Stryker writes, "in practice...

these terms usually refer to people who reject the terms transgender or trans-sexual for themselves, because they think the terms are either old-fashioned or too conceptually enmeshed in gender history" (25). Though some nonbinary or genderqueer people may feel this way, many, myself included, identify strongly with the word transgender and the abbreviated version "trans." For the trans community, it is painful to see a respected transgender theorist minimize non-binary identity and distance nonbinary-ness from transgender identity. Reading Stryker's misrepresentation of nonbinary and genderqueer people shows that identities outside the binary are misunderstood and invalidated even within the transgender community. Taking this into consideration, how do misrepresented and underrepresented nonbinary folks consume and relate to film? Oftentimes, they turn to films with crossdressing, gender bending, and binary transgender characters. Even with inaccurate portrayals of trans experience, many trans people seek out media with gender bending representations. What we find is less than satisfactory. When trans people are represented in film, they are usually depicted as monsters or used for comic relief. Though there is a wide array of film with crossdressing, transgender, and gender bending characters, the most overtly negative transgender representation tends to happen in horror film.

In horror movies, trans people are nearly always presented as a monster or se-rial killer and their actual identity is not directly addressed. So, these characters do not always use the word transgender but their roles are based on what film-makers imagine transgender people to be. Often, the monster is a murderous trans woman. Such is the case in *Sleepaway Camp* (1983) and *Dressed to Kill* (1980). The fear induced by these characters comes not only from their murderous tendencies but also from their trans identity. The intended reaction to their trans identities is an example of Kristeva's theory of abjection. Kristeva defines abjec-tion as anything identified as outside of the self. It is the things we expel from our bodies and understand as an undesirable part of our self once it is outside of us; it is vomit, piss, blood, and other vile bodily fluids. The reason she argues we are disgusted by the abject has to do with boundaries and borders: "It is thus not lack of cleanliness or health that causes abjection but what disturbs identity, system, order. What does not respect borders, positions, rules. The in-between, the ambiguous, the composite" (3). Trans women in horror films are viewed as boundary-breaking and in-between society's binary gender system. They are intended to cause discomfort because they cross this border.

Abjection is the subject of horror film. So why do people like to watch horror when it makes viewers uncomfortable? Barbara Creed argues that horror is directly connected to Kristeva's theory. Kristeva describes the corpse as the ultimate abjection in human society. Creed writes:

> In relation to horror film, it is relevant to note that several of the most popular horrific figures are 'bodies without souls' (the vampire), the 'living corpse' (the zombie) and the corpse-eater (the ghouls). Here, the horror film constructs and confronts us with the fascinating, seductive aspect of abjection (70).

There are multiple reasons why people are drawn to abjection despite it being frightening, grotesque, and even painful to watch. For Creed, the reason is the allure of reconnecting with the primal self that is unashamed of the abject and fascinated with death. For Carol Clover, however, abjection has to do with painful looking. Clover argues that horror "insists that the pleasure of looking at others in fear and pain has its origins in one's own past but not finished fear and pain" (230). So, watching horror provides a location for viewers to project their own struggles with fear, loss, and death and to be able to feel those feelings in a contained, socially acceptable manner, since it is expected that people will have emotional or frightful reactions to horror.

As much of the general population views trans people as abject, it is not surprising that trans individuals are included in horror. Trans bodies—not unlike intersex bodies, Black and Brown bodies, and disabled bodies—are breaking the comfortable boundaries of society by way of crossing gendered lines and sometimes sitting between or outside of those lines depending on hormones, surgery, and gender expression. By the definition of the abject, it makes sense that in a society that strictly constructs two genders, people who disrupt the binary in any way would be viewed as abject beings. Horror films have capitalized on this fear in society by way of the murderous trans woman trope.

Both *Sleepaway Camp* (1983) and *Dressed to Kill* (1980) exemplify the view that trans women are abject figures. In *Sleepaway Camp* (1983), there is a serial killer on the loose at a children's summer camp. Throughout the movie, killings are shown with the murderer out of frame. The big twist ending is that the killer is actually one of the young campers who we believed was a girl but is actually assigned male at birth and was forced to dress as a girl by their abusive guardian who wanted a daughter. So, though the actual identity of the character is not known, when it is revealed that someone presenting as a young girl has a penis, the viewer is supposed to be shocked and scared. In the horror genre, gender reveal is a famous scene because it is supposed to be a big, terrifying plot twist.

In *Dressed to Kill* (1980), transgender identity is equated with mental illness. The killer is transgender and bipolar. When they are manic, they dress as a woman and kill people. When depressed, they present as a man. Being trans is equated with being mentally ill, which creates a problematic and false presentation of trans identity. The viewer is meant to find the "man" in the dress to be scary. I use quotes around "man" because we do not know the true identity of the character, though their psychologist mentions that they want gender confirmation surgery without specifying how they identify their gender.

The warped representation of trans women in horror films has real-world implications, which are addressed by May Valdivia Rude in her article on the subject. Misrepresentations affects viewers because "when they hear that someone is a trans woman, they have a list of characters that are lumped into a general category of 'women who are really men' and that category is filled with psychopaths and killers" (Valdivia Rude). Inaccurate depictions can lead to people thinking of trans women as less than human. In their misguided minds, they become monstrous beings made of only the abject. They will likely apply this faulty logic to other trans people as well, viewing all trans bodies as fear-inducing due to their nonconformity. Misguided views like these lead to violence. The National Coalition of Anti-Violence Programs notes, "misinformed and negative imagery often lead[s] to increases in violence against particular populations" (Kinkead). To mitigate such misinformed views, a trans gaze is essential to critique cissexist films.

Film needs a nonbinary trans gaze because a majority of the mainstream representations we have, particularly in horror film, contribute to rhetoric that can feed into transphobia and induce violence against trans people. On top of a shifted gaze, complete inclusion of trans people requires concrete changes in the film industry and more theorizing on the subject of transgender people in film. Of the little theory available on trans folks in film, nonbinary people are often excluded the conversations altogether, hence my emphasis on a nonbinary and trans gaze.

What we need from films, though, is not simply less violent representation. We crave films with more accurate and complex trans experiences, ideally involving trans people throughout the production process. For example, *Ma Vie en Rose* (1997), though full of sad moments, shows hope and realistic emotion without demonizing or invalidating its trans main character. Future films must tackle what it's like to live as a trans woman of color, what it's like to be nonbinary, what it's like to be a trans man. We deserve to see ourselves in goofy comedies, slashers, superhero movies, and cheesy romantic comedies. Trans-forward media developed with the trans gaze would not only benefit trans people. While trans people would benefit from decreased violence and stigma, cisgender people, too would be able to see the possibilities of gender outside the binary.

References

Clover, C. J. (2015). *Men, Women, and Chain Saws: Gender in the Modern Horror Film - Updated Edition* (Princeton Classics, 73) (Revised ed.). Princeton University Press.

Jancovich, M. (2009). Horror and the Monstrous-Feminine: An Imaginary Abjection. In M. Jancovich (Ed.), *Horror, the Film Reader* (pp. 67–76). Routledge.

Evans, C., & Gammon, L. (1995). The Gaze Revisited, or Reviewing Queer Viewing. In P. Burston, P. B. Nfa, & C. Richardson (Eds.), *A Queer Romance: Lesbians, Gay Men, and Popular Culture* (pp. 13–56). Routledge.

hooks, b. (2014). *Black Looks: Race and Representation* (2nd ed.). Routledge.

Kinkead, M. (2011, September 14). Negative Transgender Imagery in Horror Films Explored. GLAAD. https://www.glaad.org/2008/10/23/negative-images-of-transgender-people-in-film-explored

Kristeva, J., & Roudiez, L. (1982). *Powers of Horror: An Essay on Abjection (European Perspectives Series)* (Reprint ed.). Columbia University Press.

Mulvey, L. (2009). Visual Pleasure and Narrative Cinema. In *Visual and Other Pleasures (Language, Discourse, Society)* (2nd ed., pp. 14–27). Palgrave Macmillan.

Stryker, S. (2017). *Transgender History, second edition: The Roots of Today's Revolution* (Seal Studies) (2nd ed.). Seal Press.

Valdivia Rude, M. (2021, April 28). *Who's Afraid Of The Big, Bad Trans Woman? On Horror and Transfemininity.* Autostraddle. https://www.autostraddle.com/whos-afraid-of-the-big-bad-trans-woman-on-horror-and-transfemininity-198212/

LOVE, CHAOS, AND FREDDY KRUEGER

AMBER RW KNAPP

When you ask an avid horror fan what the first horror movie they ever watched was, they're usually quick and eager to answer. Someone's first horror experience can be recalled with the same fondness that one remembers their first concert, or maybe even their first kiss. My first and most vivid memory of horror was a singular image of Freddy Kreuger on the back of the *A Nightmare on Elm Street 4: The Dream Master* VHS. Adorned in surgical scrubs, the green light accentuating every curve, and every groove of the burns that cover his face and hands. I don't know why that alone grossed me out as much as it did, but that image was burned into my brain (pun only sort of intended). It bothered me so much that I rearranged the tapes on the edge of the shelf, so I didn't have to see it whenever I came up the steps.

If my memory serves me right, the first time I saw *Evil Dead II* was when I was in the sixth grade. The outrageous splatter gore and slapstick comedy on top of an ancient demonic book with words no one could understand went right over my head. Next to *Evil Dead II*, I have vague memories of seeing Stephen King's AC/DC-fueled movie *Maximum Overdrive*, as it was one that my parents had seen on a date at a drive-in, so it played on our TV periodically. Though those two were technically the first two horror movies I ever saw, I don't count them "officially" because I didn't begin my train wreck of a dive into the genre for a little while yet.

I fell down the rabbit hole of the horror genre in seventh or eighth grade when the second story of my small house in the city became my "hang out" spot. While it was still piled with storage totes and various shit, including a bean bag chair for the longest time, it had been cleared enough for me to have a spot to put a futon and a TV. We were a bit behind on the times, so aside from the most basic of DVD players one could buy, most of the movies I had were still being watched on a VCR. On one of the shelves of tapes were three of the *A Nightmare on Elm Street* films; the first, the third, *Dream Warriors*, and the fourth,

Dream Master. I didn't quite get why Part 2 *Freddy's Revenge* was skipped over, but I suppose it would make sense to me these years later after various events and observations.

My best friend at the time let's call her "Anna", was over at my house all the time. Hangouts, weekend sleepovers where we tried to copy My Chemical Romance's Revenge-era make-up, all the time. During one such hangout, we were trying to pick a movie from my shelves to watch. I suppose that day was "the day, and I picked up *Wes Craven's A Nightmare on Elm Street.* I knew I was in for seeing more of that morphed and burned face that had severely creeped me out. I looked at Anna, being my best friend, and admitted to her how much it scared me, and if I had gotten too scared to finish watching it, I knew she wouldn't give me shit for chickening out.

The movie begins, the audience sees Tina's first nightmare, is introduced to Nancy, Rod, and Glenn, then returns to Tina's house for the second on-screen nightmare. After Freddy mockingly growls at Tina, **"THIS is God,"** he runs after her. For those who have seen this movie, you know how he runs- bouncing from side to side like he's on a poorly drawn hop-scotch path and waving his hands in the air like he just don't care. It's just comical. That sneering face cackling and mocking his future victim, and, as we know, the humor only got goofier and darker after the first entry of the slasher franchise.

I had seen this face for so long, and it occupied my mind so long, only for me to look at the movie and be like, "Oh wow. That wasn't so bad. I want more of this kind of stuff."

As I frequented my local Family Video and Hollywood Video to seek out more horror movies, I was also seeking out my first real romantic interest. I was past schoolyard crushes and wanted to date someone. The first person to tell me that they cared about me in such a way was my best friend at the time, Anna. While the circumstances of the relationship were toxic as hell, I was too young to stand up for myself and fell into puppy love (if you want to call it that) and the relationship lasted about a year. While friends at school were accepting of my same-sex relationship, I wasn't as lucky at home. Horror movies are a way for us to seek out chaos in a way that we can control. When you look for a new horror movie to watch, you wonder, "Would this scare me or not?" When you look at someone and are thinking about coming out to them, you wonder, "Would they react positively or negatively?" After my initial coming out meeting a more negative reaction, I began seeking out the horror that I could control.

If you're a person in the LGBTQ+ community, you're probably very accustomed to over-thinking. It's part of your own safety and well-being. You have to pay extra attention to your environment. If you're driving through a town and see ignorant right wing nut signs left and right, then you know not to stop there, no matter how bad you might want to stop for snacks, or to use the bathroom. As a member of the LGBTQ+ community or a woman, you're almost taught to overthink certain situations. You're taught not to go out alone at night, or when you do, you walk with your keys or mace in hand. You overhear harsh and hateful language that teaches you who you want to avoid when given the chance. You overhear family members saying homophobic, transphobic, racist, or sexist things, and it teaches you who you can't trust.When you're a part of the LGBTQ+ community, you're never really done "coming out." It can be done explicitly or subtly, up-front or after a while of knowing someone. Meeting new people or even starting a new job can start the coming out process all over again. That's before you even take into account that sexuality and gender are both very fluid things. Maybe you come out as gay, lesbian, or bisexual and that's that. Or perhaps your heart and feelings shift over time. No one way is more or less valid than another.

I've been through most of the letters of the acronym as my feelings developed. From bisexual to lesbian, to bisexual, to pansexual, to queer, to queer asexual. The last one is a more recent development, having "clicked" for me during the time I started typing out my first draft of this essay. Thus, I had to do another round of "coming out" to those closest to me and answer any questions that came along with it. My initial coming out years ago was not the most pleasant experience, as it wasn't on my own terms, and I'm still feeling the ripple effects of that to this day. It made me anxious to communicate a lot of things that were deeply affecting me, including things that had nothing to do with my sexuality. It was uninvited and unwelcome chaos in my life.

Sometimes the chaos is inviting. Taglines on movie posters or in trailers such as "The scariest movie since The Exorcist" or "The Netflix movie so scary that people can't make it through" where they try to appeal to the daredevil fan in you. If you're lucky, you can come across inviting (and much less chaotic) queer or trans-friendly spaces. Many queer and trans horror fans seek out both cringe and comfort. We look for horror movies that scare and entertain us as we search for an accepting community. I'm thankful I've found an accepting niche of queer horror beings, from podcasters to writers, directors, and oodles of other fans.

While a lot of the horror community is LGBTQ+ friendly, there are assholes still out there. There are still people out there who don't think that horror movies should be queer or even political when horror movies have been innately both since the inception of the genre. We usually don't seek out such spiteful party-poopers, but they come in uninvited through social media. Social media has been a blessing and curse, let's be honest. While we are bombarded with homophobic and transphobic comments and other violent acts, we can meet some of the coolest and most loving people who we might not have even known existed if not for social media. I might not have found LGBTQ+ horror podcasts or found other queer horror content creators if I didn't fall down the rabbit hole of the internet. I'm not sure if I would have ended up learning all of these things about myself if I never learned to roll with the punches/ride the rollercoaster/whatever metaphor you'd like to insert here, or if I never learned to take in and embrace the chaos while also seeking it out.

TOWARDS A RADICAL TRANS FUTURE IN THE SLASHER FILM

RC JARA

Content Warning: transphobia

In the 1987 essay "Her Body, Himself: Gender in the Slasher Film", Carol J. Clover establishes the final girl: a lone survivor who must navigate a psychosexual hellscape known as "The Terrible Place" to fight the monster. Often fought in a house or other grounds consecrated by the monster's trauma and repression, this is the cumulative test by which her resilience is proved. This archetype has given horror devotees a language with which to identify survivors in a cinematic realm, and in a real-world context. Where Clover's assessments merit push-back, however, is how she defines the relationship between the subgenre and its viewership, and in her reliance on a gender binary. Clover's essay contains a rigid position on gender identity from a psychoanalytic standpoint. According to her, the final girl is a mechanism for men to project "cross-gender" fantasies of themselves. The archetype, she asserts, nullifies the existence of male heroes but doesn't serve an audience of women. Clover also troublingly diagnoses "gender confusion" in male viewers, blaming them for a supposed cultural usurpation of womanhood through a vicarious exploration of "deviant impulses." In other words, slashers predominantly exist as a perverted operation to push back on the gains of second-wave feminism.

Suffice to say that while the final girl may be empowering, the archetype's development is severely regressive. Trans history has seen incalculable erasure in the form of libraries lost to fascist regimes and horrifically antiquated medical science. This woefully abridged historical context doesn't even begin to cover the wreckage of colonialism. And as of 2019, the WHO has only just begun the process of declassifying being trans as a mental disorder. That said, Clover's pathologizing of straight cisgender men in horror is a drop in the bucket. But transphobia as a form of toxicity in the media is persistent. As a trans femme horror writer for whom final girls have been formative, I can say that my personal connection wasn't based on a need to usurp womanhood. In a sense, I owe early moments of clarity to them and to the creators who worked to bring them to life. Even so, it should be burned in people's psyche that our existence cannot and should not be pathologized through movie characters. Especially when there is much more value investigating gender identity in a critically underappreciated subgenre.

The monster/survivor dynamic has been a center of fascination for me in my own reading of slasher films. This framework has been popularized by Clover. Yet, even by the time her writing was published (and primarily during the post-modernist slasher boom of the mid-1990s) the absolutist position of the monster as an abject being seems flat. Clover supports this idea with anecdotal material from filmmakers like Alfred Hitchcock and Brian De Palma, whose most popular works have imbued villainous characters with repressive characteristics. *Psycho*, whose killer's motives are ham-fistedly explained at the end, is generally regarded as the progenitor of the slasher, and *Dressed to Kill* is one of the earliest films to investigate trans issues for better and worse. Clover's usurpation narrative appears solvent if viewed from the strict analytical framework of men forcibly assuming women's roles, or visa-versa. But, thankfully, we have seen horror scholarship free the monster from their status as a non-subject and the sole survivor from the grip of reductive social categorization.

In his study "When the Final Girl is Not a Girl: Reconsidering the Gender Binary in the Slasher Film", Dr. Jeremy Maron provides a fluid reading of what he calls the Final Subject. The study deconstructs Clover's work through several popular films which utilize the relationship between the "subject" and the "abject" to tell their story. That is, the journey a survivor must make to have control of their destiny and the "unlivable place" in which the monster/killer is forced to dwell, respectively. This paradigm can be used to view slashers on a surface level. We watch a Final Subject wander through a mess of bodies before meeting her depersonalized tormentor face-to-face. As Dr. Maron investigates the Final Subject and their relationship to the monster, however, he concludes that it is more beneficial to erode the border separating them, thereby, making the impersonal personal.

Dr. Maron counters the Cloverian binary system with Jesse Walsh (Mark Patton) in *A Nightmare On Elm Street 2: Freddy's Revenge*. Using Judith Butler's conception of the "constitutive outside," he categorizes categorizes Jesse as a Final Subject who nonetheless resides unfavorably on the periphery. Unlike Nancy, Jesse's status as a subject depends heavily on inclusion in heteronormative spaces. His perceived feminine traits place him in hostile territory among other men. He is an anomaly in the subgenre who harbors the traits of a survivor, and he becomes a vessel for violence. In this sequel, Freddy warps reality from the outside as he and Jesse live as one. Jesse is a subject whose wants and needs are communicated empathetically until Freddy, previously lurking in the abject darkness of the unconscious, becomes an inextricable part of him. Dr. Maron delineates this ambiguous space with instances where Jesse's fears have resulted in killings, and his subsequent feelings of remorse.

In its finale, the film viciously unravels any sense of closure for Jesse. On a bus ride to school, Freddy resurfaces for one last scare to kill everyone around him. Whether this occurs in a dreamscape is beside the point. The open-ended nature of the film solidifies the tether between monster and survivor, eschewsing popular heteronormative readings before the final girl was fully defined as an archetype. Homophobic reaction to the film notwithstanding, *Freddy's Revenge* remains one of the most challenging sequels in any slasher franchise. The fluidity exemplified by Jesse in the overlap between him and Freddy is perhaps more important for slashers today than it was during the initial boom. Recent films like *Tragedy Girls* and *Lucky* have both taken this concept to explore themes of grief, loss, and empowerment in the face of crushing circumstances. Final Subjects have always rendered these messages tangible for me. However, in the monstrous side of slashers lies an anarchic possibility that continues to push the subgenre forward.

In Dr. Joelle Ruby Ryan's dissertation "Reel Gender: Examining The Politics Of Trans Images In Film And Media", the concept of embodying monstrosity as a means of empowerment is thoroughly considered. They contend that in the face of ugly tropes like the "she-male psycho," monstrosity can be embraced without being used to cause violence to or inspire fear within trans communities (Ryan, 2009, p. 231). Sowing a culture for this perspective to thrive allows trans people the room to channel their insecurities within a horror film without being confronted by sensationalized portrayals of themselves. When I began research into this essay, I hoped to cover films that were either underseen or had gone underwritten about. As an outlier within its own subgenre, however, I could not shake *Freaky*—a slasher that reinterprets the magical body-swapping premise of Mary Rogers's *Freaky Friday*. The film discards allegory in its entirety by presenting trans themes forward, and despite a global pandemic, its critical and commercial success solidifies it as one of the most visible horror projects to do so in recent times.

In the film, protagonist Millie Kessler (Kathryn Newton) walks a fluid line between monstrosity and heroism. Millie is a bullied high school student who is at-tacked by a serial killer known as The Butcher (Vince Vaughn) late after a football game. Waiting for a ride home in the dark, she is chased and tackled onto the chool's football field where the two are simultaneously cut by the killer's weapon, La Dola—a cursed blade that acts as a broker of spirits between vessels. The next morning, on Friday the 13th, sees the swapped pair attempt to carefully navigate the other's body. While Millie races to switch back before midnight or else be permanently trapped as a wanted fugitive, the Butcher enjoys his newfound cover and makes the switch difficult through horrific acts of violence.

The opportunity to launch a dialogue was limitless in *Freaky*. Even before her consciousness is transferred onto The Butcher, Millie displays alienation from her own body. The clothing she wears cover her chest and her curves, for which Millie is rebuked by the film's only openly gay character. Millie's extracurricular activity involves a presence during football games, but not as a cheerleader. She opts for the gender-neutral option of the school mascot. Regardless, she is sexually harassed in ways that refer to her genitals. Yet the script never capitalizes on most of what is insinuated or bluntly relayed to us about Millie's struggles with identity and gender presentation. The film wastes potential in a character whose insecure sense of self defies a typical coming-of-age story. The specificity of Millie's pain is recognizable in how Newton plays the role and the way she is framed in comparison to other characters we assume are cisgender. This would have been less concerning if the film had not explicitly baited trans viewers.

Interestingly, *Freaky's* theatrical one-sheet displays a provocative image of The Butcher in possession of Millie covered in shaving cream with a large blade pressed against her cheek. Copies of the film's Blu-Ray are marked as the "Killer Switch Edition", playing on the sexual and gender implications of the word "switch." Neither idea gets the space to breathe in their profundity. It is a frustrating watch because the angst of our protagonist is never addressed past a superficial level. But the story's worst tendencies lie in being overly dependent on transmisogyny from the transformation onwards. To begin with, the idea that trans people are body-swapped, or are the spirit of another gender trapped in the wrong body, is a consis-tent weapon used against communities. In *Freaky*, these harmful talking points are parroted by nebulous characters in moments of self-awareness. But as is the case with the film as a whole, a deeper reading is suffocated by the central gag.

When Millie first wakes up as The Butcher, she frantically turns to an addict in the building they are squatting in and asks, "Do I look like a girl?" To which the man replies, "I wanna feel like a girl! I'll suck your dick!" The joke is meant to land on the addict who is looking for a fix so potent that he too will suffer gender dysphoria. As Millie immediately faces a hostile environment, the film's veneer of empathy begins to crumble. The hostility is partly justified by the fact that The Butcher's face is revealed to the public on TV, yet it nonetheless resembles the experience of taking up space as a non-passing trans femme. This imagery bears an uncomfortable weight in isolation, but the script compounds the ridicule by placing a jarring emphasis on using the "correct" pronouns for Millie and The Butcher, respectively. Still, the irreverent qualities of this humor are non-exis-tent. Though genre films generally thrive off bad taste, there is an off-hand joke about misgendering that derogatorily refers to one of the characters as "woke" that isn't even refreshingly offensive.

Freaky continuously asks its trans audience members to participate in a story where both subjects' concerns are suppressed no matter how visible. Its stream-lining of slasher tropes make the film one of the most accessible to modern viewers, but it fails to meaningfully capture the oppressive confines of its own world. The attitude it carries gives the impression of a need to smash and re-build. But compared to 2017's *Tragedy Girls*, a film with an open disdain for the heteronormative rituals of a small-town existence, this film feels empty. Popular wisdom would say to make space for more than one entry in teen-centric horror. The trouble with *Freaky* is that it stops itself short of breathing life to a story that has gone undertold for decades. Among the film's most disappointing pitfalls are lines of dialogue that manage to be introspective without a pay-off. Take, for instance, this bit of double entendre:

"You can't be walking around with those clothes and that face," says Millie's friend.

While this line offers a desperately needed pass at self-reflection, "I feel oddly empowered being in this body...It's ridiculous but I guess when you're someone like me and you've been bullied most of your life and put down a lot, it does feel kinda good to feel strong for once," says Millie.

Once Millie is able to switch back, The Butcher asks one of the most profound questions of any monster in slasher history:

"You got your body back. Why aren't you happy?"

This is indeed loaded. After the final switch, Millie is still fundamentally unhappy with her appearance. With her role among her friends and at home. In her inability to connect with others at school and to her love interest. Millie's coming-of-age story reflects a queer-trans point-of-view so poignantly at times, it's nauseating to watch her wander around in The Butcher's body just for laughs. Not even the kiss Millie shares with her male love interest, while in the body of The Butcher, is particularly elucidating. Millie's struggle is muted in a film that insists on focalizing transness. She doesn't get to savor the freedom that monstrosity grants the disempowered survivor. Nothing that comes from The Butcher affirm parts of himself in a female-presenting body either. Each of them gets to know the other intimately, but an incurious script ultimately refuses to develop the transness clawing at the screen.

The film's ending sees our two leads revert back to their original state without drawing much insight into their monster-survivor dynamic. Rather than further the conversation that Jesse had with his own body in *Freddy's Revenge*, the writing banks on dehumanizing associations with transness to sell its humor. It reinforces a gender and moral binary that readily invites comparisons to the Cloverian notion of psychosexual deviancy. Despite it being rooted in an outsider perspective, what truly damns the film is its inability to recognize the distinctness of being trans as a struggle apart from accepted queerness. There doesn't seem to be a reason, for example, why the film couldn't have centered the anxieties of its one openly gay character and still come away with the same message. Instead, *Freaky* transposes vague angst onto a vulnerable character whose arc is never given proper shape. There is no room for complex ideas of being trans. This is an omission so glaring that older, "she-male psycho" oriented films like *Sleepaway Camp* and *Dressed to Kill* are (lamentably) more beneficial to understanding trans (mis)representation in horror.

Dr. Ryan's study of the "she-male psycho myth" explains that its role in horror films has the potential to influence trans narratives that challenge the status quo. As a fan of genre sleaze, I admit the most openly wretched films can be surprisingly curious and enjoyable in isolation. But there comes a point when finding one that just barely scrapes the surface of possibility wears my patience thin. And these films too often validate the insecurities and fears of cisgender people. Dr. Ryan writes: "[t]here is an almost maniacal level of hatred used that is about more than just killing the person. The violence becomes symbolic: it is about killing everything that the person represents" (Ryan, 2009, p. 190). It is this willful lack of humanity that further emphasizes my dismay at *Freaky*. It dangles instances of real-world violence in front of us then asks us to laugh about it. To accept the indignity of seeing trans issues pulled to the forefront, only to relegate them back to the abject through ridicule. To affirm a cisgender public's right to see some of us as body swappers. Without this gag to fall back on, there isn't much of a point to the film aside from being a thought experiment.

In slashers, trans "representation" has been fraught with violence and willful misunderstanding. For Dr. Ryan, the ideology of a given film does not neatly coincide with external violence on marginalized people. However, they insist that images "congeal over time and take on the mode of 'master texts' which function to improperly inform humans about diversity in the social world" (Ryan, 2009, p. 235). In my journey through queer horror history, I cherish Dr. Ryan's work. There are films that carry harmful trans stereotypes we wouldn't know how to recognize if dedicated historians like them did not establish the necessary critical language. Whether *Freaky* is an example of a film that shapes perception on transness in the negative has yet to be seen. At the time of this writing, it is only a year old and has many vocal fans. I certainly wouldn't argue for it or any other film to be censored or withdrawn from conversation regardless. But the struggle as a marginalized fan working from the fringe is that most people prefer things to remain uncomplicated, especially when coming from the ever-inscrutable cisgender white imagination.

Even in the transgressive genre of horror, queerness and transness must be smuggled by filmmakers or unearthed after the fact. Otherwise, we are made to suffer material that masks itself as radical but is functionally conservative. It is a total shame that the model of film production is less than hospitable to trans creators. Those who do get work in the medium, to produce personal stories of their becoming no less, face steep challenges. Droughts can be dispiriting, and I commend the slasher subgenre for continuing to evolve past binaries. We can always count on horror to deliver where more delicate genres fail. But until queerness and transness can be the subject of slashers without gimmicks, scraps will be treated as such. I'd rather have 100 trans-led, scripted, directed, produced slasher films bump head-to-head with one another in joyous cacophony than one that revels in trans-panic humor almost half a century past its expiration date. As we work towards a radical trans future on screen, I hope to see multitudinous characterizations of trans people grace our films and behind the scenes.

References

Clover, C. J. (1987). Her Body, Himself: Gender in the Slasher Film. Representations, Special Issue(20), 187-228.

Clover, C. J. (1992). Men, Women, and Chain Saws: Gender in the Modern Horror Film. Princeton, N.J: Princeton University Press.

Maron, J. (2015). When the Final Girl is Not a Girl: Reconsidering the Gender Binary in the Slasher Film. Offscreen, 19 (1). https://offscreen.com/view/reconsidering-the-final-girl

Ruby Ryan, J. (2009). Reel Gender: Examining The Politics Of Trans Images In Film And Media. [Doctoral dissertation, Bowling Green State University].

OUR CONTRIBUTORS

Amber RW Knapp

Amber R.W. Knapp (they/them) jumped into the deep end when it came to writing about the horror genre. They are the creator of the horror blog Another One For The Fire", a nod to the closing line of George A. Romero's Night Of The Living Dead. Their work can also be found in We Are Horror online magazine and Neon Splatter website. They live in Michigan with their rambunctious puppy, Brody.

Ashley D

Ashlina is a Latinx content creator, model & artist who loves Halloween all year & exploring deeper elements within the horror genre. What once was a fun way to spend time on the weekends has turned into her love & passion.

Bernadetta F

Bernadetta F is a life long fan of horror in all its various forms, living in the United Kingdom. They are currently undertaking a PhD at the University of Lincoln researching the various connections between Moral Panics, censorship in non-authoritarian regimes and the new media landscape. In their spare time Bernie is looking to help share LGBT+ stories as well as help people get into film-making on a local level. They previously undertook a Masters in International Relations at the University of Leeds and a Bachelors degree in History & Film at the University of Hull. Bernie also occasion makes videos both for fun and for work.

Blayne Waterloo

Blayne (she/her) is a writer and web designer from Central Pennsylvania. She has a degree and background in both journalism and creative writing and enjoys rambling about trauma, mental health, and her passion for the horror genre. Blayne hosts the podcast Silver Scream Queens with her best friends, and can often be found gushing over movies and television on Twitter.

Catherine E. Benstead

Catherine is an Australian based Sociologist with an insane love for blood, guts, and gore. She is the founder of Hear Us Scream and contributes a monthly column "Horrorology" where she examines sociological and criminological perspectives of horror movies. Catherine has a deep love for the horror community and is passionate about providing a space for horror lovers to come together and share their love for the genre. On her off days, Catherine spends time with her spooky nieces, waiting on her calico cat Pickles hand and foot, and hosting the horror movies podcast, Thank God It's Friday!

Destiny Kelly

Destiny is a visual horror artist and filmmaker from Southern California. She creates a variety of mixed media traditional and digital artwork inspired by the horror genre. In 2020, Destiny received her Bachelor's Degree from Long Beach State University's Film and Electronic Arts program, with a specialization in Production Design. Outside of doing art department related work on film sets, she has a passion for writing and directing her own independent horror short films.

Dulce Maria

Dulce was born and raised in Miami, Florida but currently lives in Atlanta where she works in higher education helping students. Dulce has a degree in English Lit (minor philosophy) and would have to say that her favourite author is Shakespeare though her interests are pretty fluid. Dulce says that horror has prepared her for the world in many ways and she's still deciding if that's a good or a bad thing! Dulce can deal with anything as long as it's not 100 zombies running after her!

Dylyn C.S

Dylyn, also known as Dylyn C.S., is a die-hard genre fan and film buff based in Washington state. As a queer, Jewish, chronically ill, and neurodivergent woman, she enjoys analyzing film through the intersections of these identities. In addition to her monthly column for Hear Us Scream ("Holy Terrors," an exploration of Jewish talent in horror), she has written for other genre-analysis sites like Monster Thoughts and Slay Away. Currently, she and her partner are cultivating a video project called "PNW Halloween," which will be a year-round dedication to cozy, autumnal ambience. Along with her horror adventures, however, she is working on a thriller-based project in her spare time and hopes to one day achieve her master's degree in Film History. An avid poetry-lover, she also dreams of someday publishing a poetry book, as her love of writing first blossomed from her love of poetry.

Elecia Page

Elecia Page writes spooky tales and ghost stories. She is the Assistant Director of Out For Blood, a queer horror film festival based in Cambridgeshire, UK. Elecia enjoys reading gothic novels and roller skating (although not at the same time). She lives in the fens with her partner and a cat named Kimba.

E.L. King

E. L. King (also known as Enola Lugosi) is a horror lover, writer and critic. They host the Slay Away horror podcast and are the Editor-in-Chief of horror media outlet SlayAwayWithUs.com. Their recent projects include voice acting as main character Ada in Fossil Games new game Sunshine Manor releasing October 28th on all platforms and an upcoming narrative podcast exploring urban legends, myths and folk horror. They reside in the horror hub of Austin, Texas, host a horror gaming channel on Twitch and YouTube and enjoy chatting about horror on Instagram, Twitter and TikTok.

Gena Radcliffe

Gena Radcliffe is the co-host of the horror podcast Kill by Kill, and she is a writer and managing editor at the film and television website The Spool. Her work has been featured in Daily Grindhouse, Anatomy of a Scream, F This Movie and Grim Magazine. A native of Atlantic City, New Jersey, the weirdest place on Earth, she lives in Brooklyn with her family and one extremely shy cat.

Hari Berrow

Hari is a Welsh and working-class writer and postgraduate researcher. She is currently pursuing a PhD in Creative and Critical Writing at Cardiff University, exploring ways of using horror to create scripted presentations of mental ill-health within the horror genre. Hari recently completed The Other Room's Emerging Writers programme in association with Bad Wolf Studios, and her work has been featured in T'Art Magazine and Keep on Writing 2020. She has lectured online for The Folklore Podcast and Rural Gothic Conference and has worked with various universities and institutions to offer creative workshops. In 2020, she hosted monthly Horrorthons and, between May and December, watched 245 horror films—she deeply regrets this decision.

Jack Van Tuyle

Jack Van Tuyle is a visual artist, currently living in California with their partner and two cats. They were born in 1997 and will probably die around 2077. Their interests include loud noises, violent movies, and fashion.

Jerry Sampson

Jerry Sampson is a horror writer, screenwriter, and film analyst. Her love for film and the horror genre leads her to explore and question the darkness that lies in the shadows of human existence. She studies the concept of inherited trauma and finds this theme coming up consciously and unconsciously in much of her work. She has a monthly feature on the Rue Morgue website called Beautiful Filth which focuses on Extreme Horror films through the female gaze. Jerry is the Editor-in-Chief of Buckman Journal and she writes for Ghouls Magazine, Moving Pictures Film Club, Hear Us Scream, and other publications. She is currently in pre-production on her first short film, In Dreams.

Jenni Holtz

Jenni Holtz is a Chicago-based LGBTQ+ health researcher, illustrator, and writer passionate about work centering the transgender community. Body horror is their favorite horror subgenre, as it captures their experience of being trans and disabled. Raw (2016), Suspiria (2018), The Skin I Live In (2011), and Possessor (2020) are some of their favorites in the genre. Their writing has been published at Autostraddle, In Their Own League, Flip Screen, Film Daze, Screen Queens, Loose Lips, and Restless Mag. When they're not sketching or typing, they can be found sitting under the nearest tree with a good book and a cold brew in hand.

Jessica Scott

Jessica Scott is a freelance horror journalist with a passion for discussing the ways that the genre explores gender, queer identity, and mental health. She has bylines online and in print for outlets such as Film Cred, Daily Grindhouse, Nightmarish Conjurings, Grim Magazine, Screen Queens, and Ghouls Magazine. She is also the co-host of the horror film podcast ReHeated.

KC Amira

KC Amira Calvo is a PhD researcher looking at the relationship between Reagan era cultural conservatism and child autonomy in 1980s biological horror cinema. She is the author of Heavy Metal Coffin, The Ivory Brush and several other short horror fiction pieces. Her passion project, Horror Chromatic, is a website dedicated to discussing diversity in the horror community and uplifting BIPOC fans and creatives alike. She lives in Brighton, England with her three cats.

Kristen

Kristen, aka Chucky's Side Chick , has had a love for all things horror since the age of 17. She has passionately been a part of the DFWTO podcast since January of 2019. She especially loves watching horror films and enjoying all things creepy and spooky during the fall season. Being from the Midwest has its perks! She hopes to one day be able to run her podcast with her best friend as a full time career!

Kyasia Fields

Kyasia Fields (KyFx) (she/they/them) is a Houston Based Special Effects Makeup Artist , Podcaster and Black Horror Scholar. They are the founder of KyFx Horror Group , a multimedia platform support inclusion in the Horror genre while accentuating the importance of Black Horror creatives and the Host of Monstrosities Voice Horror Untouched Podcast , the podcast for Black Horror By Black Horror.

Lucy Derry-Holmes

Lucy is a horror podcaster, writer and Twitch streamer based in Scotland with a passion for historical horror cinema, intersectional feminism and analysing queer theory.

Marina Garrido

Marina is a 23-year-old book reviewer who got her bachelor's degree in Literature from The University of Campinas, a public university in Brazil that is ranked among the top universities in Latin America. She has been fluent in English since the age of 16 and achieved the final Cambridge certification: The Certificate of Proficiency in English at 21. Currently, she's getting an MBA degree in Marketing at Fundação Getúlio Vargas and intends to go into the publishing business. Marina was featured in the first issue of Outsider - A Stephen King Zine and was a guest on the Chat Sematary podcast. You can find her reviews on the Hear Us Scream website and her Goodreads (user: 19165136-marina-garrido)

RC Jara

RC Jara (she/they) is a Latine content-creator. Their genre-focused work comprises podcasts, reviews, editorials, and filmmaker interviews. Apart from contributing to Hear Us Scream, they are currently a featured columnist on Dread Central ("Spins and Needles") and developing projects for the Anatomy Of A Scream Pod Squad Network. Outside of film writing, RC has earned their BA in Mass Communication and a Minor in Sociology.

Rebecca MaCallum

A horror scholar and film journalist, Rebecca specialises in writing think-pieces that dissect and analyse the films of the genre. As well as contributing articles for The Evolution of Horror, Zobo with a Shotgun, Grim Magazine and JumpCut Online she also has a four-part exploration focusing on the Women of the Jack the Ripper films with Rue Morgue, an ongoing series on Women in Hitchcock's films with Moving Pictures film Club and is due to release her first pocketbook in 2022.

S.C. Parris (Editor)

S.C. Parris is the author of the DARK WORLD SERIES & horror short story, A NIGHT OF FRIVOLITY. She is currently writing the sixth and final book in her dark fantasy/horror series, and is working on a new book simultaneously. She hosts the horror podcast, Monster Thoughts where she invites guests in the horror community to talk their favorite monsters, and can be seen streaming on Twitch when she isn't valeting for her professional wrestling husband.

Sam Whitaker

Sam Whitaker is the Festival Director of Out For Blood, a queer horror film festival based in Cambridgeshire, UK. Sam identitfies as non-binary and uses they/them pronouns. They hold a bachelors degree in Media Studies and are happiest when watching a film at the cinema or playing video games with friends. You can find Out For Blood at @outforbloodfilmfest on Instagram.

Violet Burns (Editor)

Violet is a freaky feminist with an unsettling volume of doll parts in her Southern California home. When she's not terrorizing patrons at haunted attractions dressed as God knows what, she teaches English as a Second Language and gets way too excited about verb tenses. She has a passion for helping others tell their stories and is incredibly lucky to serve as Co-Editor of Hear Us Scream. Violet has a soft spot for low-budget, independent horror, particularly found footage. Her graduate studies focused on phallocentric nineteenth century medical rhetoric surrounding women and madness, and she will one day own a fainting couch. She's the proud mother of two spherical Ranchu goldfish and an alarming number of plants.

Zoë Rose Smith

Zoë Rose Smith is a film journalist specialising in anything extreme, with a penchant for nasty, gory and controversial horror films and books. She is the founder of Zobo With A Shotgun website, podcast and YouTube. She is also the founder and Editor-in-Chief of Ghouls Magazine. You can find her work on Second Sight's The Guest release, Moving Pictures Film Club, Beyond Horror: The History and Sub-Culture of Red Films, Teen Screams documentary, We Are Horror, Scream Horror Magazine, The Evolution of Horror podcast, Mad About Horror, Jumpcut Online and Scream the Horror Magazine.

THANK YOU

Thank you to the following people who supported our project on KickStarter. Without you, we wouldn't have gotten the wheels turning on this big beautiful piece of art. We appreciate your support and love.

Thank you to:

Ryan Betson
Brooke Bowne
Dylan Blight
DashGamer
Patrick Hamilton
Matthew James Hewson
Ned Jankovic
Amber RW Knapp
Frederick Nuti
Chris Otto
Joy Robinson
KiKi Thomas
Jeff Sparkman
Michael Waterloo
Buddy Watson
Allen Welsh
Brendan White
Johanna Wilson
Emily Wilton
Luna Wilton
Lucy Wilton

Printed in Great Britain
by Amazon